WHEN WE TEACH KINDERGARTEN CHILDREN

A Kindergarten Guidance Manual

by KATHRENE McLANDRESS TOBEY

Board of Christian Education of the Presbyterian Church
in the United States of America
Philadelphia

268
T55 W

Library of Congress Catalog Card No.: 57-8942

36043

February 1958

CONTENTS

1. Children at Four and Five Years of Age   5

2. What We Want Them to Learn in the Church 12

3. A Good Sunday for These Children 20

4. Ways of Guiding Children in Christian Growth 30

5. A Place Children Can Call Their Own 48

6. The Teacher's Use of Printed Materials 57

7. How a Kindergarten Department Is Managed 65

1. CHILDREN AT FOUR AND FIVE YEARS OF AGE

Dear Reader:

Before you read this chapter, will you try an experiment? Take paper and pencil and write as heads of columns the names of the children who bother you in your kindergarten department. Now list briefly under each name the things that each child does that are troublesome. Try to think of all possible occasions and actions in which he has offended. It may take you five minutes and it may take you twenty. But please pause here and try it.

Now make a list of some of the children you like best and usually think of as being "good boys and girls." Under their names write the things they do that make you feel this way.

The children for whom one accepts responsibility when she becomes a kindergarten teacher are very special little beings. They have lived only four or five years—some in homes that want and love them, others in a cool atmosphere of busy adults. But all of them are God's children—miracles each one. And surely he in his creation has wondrous hopes for every child born.

Usually it is the adults with whom a child lives who ruin God's wondrous hopes. Usually it is the adults with whom a child lives who nurture his holy design. It is amazing to know from today's educators[1] and scientists, who have studied thousands of children, that as early as the eighth week of a baby's life his rate of growing decreases when he does not have tender care and love from his parents. The early disposition of another baby who receives parental devotion reflects that love and joy.

In revealing himself God has used many people as his witnesses and he continues to do so today, using persons who have placed their faith in Jesus. Thus it is that believers in Christ can radiate to little children the warmth of God's love in this his wonderful world. They can use the teachings of Jesus in their work with children to interpret to them God the Father. They can teach through showing their personal dependence upon the Bible as a necessary book for everyday use. So it is, too, that the teacher can reveal what God

---

[1] Infant and Child in the Culture of Today, by Gesell and Ilg.

means to her through the way in which she reacts to and speaks about people, for a genuine understanding and appreciation of persons, old and young, good and bad, can truly teach children that God is the Father of all men.

Just as adults can reflect the love of God and Jesus to children, so can children reveal to observing adults the laws of God. For God's laws of growth are as steady and sure in human beings as in the world of nature. But many older people neglect his laws when they begin to teach children. In our eagerness to lead the child to Christ we do not see that the child is growing ever so slowly and surely according to God's pattern of growth. We do not see that in our haste we are sometimes marring God's design because we try to lead the growing child to something he is incapable of fully absorbing till he is older. He absorbs or learns that which he is able according to these laws and his stage of growing. Sometimes he surprises an adult by repeating words that would indicate he understood them and their full meaning. But the wise adult realizes that the young child is able to repeat words and phrases in a parrotlike fashion, because at four and five his ability to imitate and repeat is part of his normal growing process. He imitates the sexton to perfection in the movements necessary for pulling the heavy rope which rings the church bell. But when he is permitted actually to pull the rope, he cannot make the bell ring. His physical stature has not attained the necessary strength to produce the adult result. It is true in a similar way that the child repeats the words of an adult who tells him that Jesus died to save him from sin. This is a fact, but it is unwise to say the words to a kindergarten child, because he is not ready to appreciate the fact and it only confuses him. In conversation and questioning the child cannot explain the meaning of the words. His mental and spiritual stature has not attained the necessary growth to produce adult results. The wise teacher realizes this, and refrains from trying to teach little children that which they should learn in a later stage of growing when they can assimilate it. We should be deeply repentant if we realized that sometimes our overzealousness to teach the child more than he can understand and put to use in daily living is the cause of the child's departure from the church when he is older. We may be the cause of the boredom and indifference that descend on some children in older primary and junior years. We must constantly be aware that our kindergarten children will really learn and absorb some teachings best when they are older, and therefore we must not try to teach them the whole Bible while they are with us.

We must study God's laws of growing; we must learn what children are like when they are four and five. There is a great deal of difference between a child who has just become four and one who is five years and nine months. As much growing takes place in these twenty-one months as comes in later life over a period of fourteen or fifteen years. This makes us curious as to what happens in that short span of one year and nine months. We wonder how we as teachers can handle a group of children who have such wide differences, and furthermore how we can teach them while this rapid growth is taking place. It is stated another way by Drs. Gesell and Ilg: "The five-year-old has come a long distance on the upward, winding pathway of development. He will have to travel fifteen years more before he becomes an adult, but he has scaled the steepest ascent and has reached a sloping plateau.... He is already stamped with individuality.... Five is a nodal age; and also a kind of golden age for both parent and child. For a brief period the tides of development flow smoothly." [2]

Mothers have made these comments as they watch individual children growing in their homes. "Tom has good spells and bad spells." "No sooner does Jean go through one difficulty and we get settled down into smooth living, than it seems that something else pops up to unravel her." "I've decided that Bobby must grow in cycles— first in one thing, then in another. He has ups and downs, smooth days and rough days, and I think it must be growth."

Parents and teachers who discover the laws of growing early are better able to live intelligently with little children. They are able to live with them in such a way that the children's desires and urges to learn are not stifled. Wise adults live with children in such a way that the spirits of all of them are happy in their togetherness in spite of occasional misunderstandings. Understanding God's laws of growing makes for smoother, more contented living.

THE FOUR-YEAR-OLD

When children who have just become four are enrolled in the kindergarten department of the church school, it is easy to make certain observations of them in contrast to the older four- and the five-year-olds. They may still have some of the busy, flitting ways of the three-year-old, but most are ready to give attention to one interest for a longer time. They are usually glad to stay in the kindergarten room without mother, although they are greatly relieved to see her again at the end of the hour. They may sit down in the block corner to build where other children are, but they build their own structures; they may join the group in the housekeeping corner, but they play independently of the older ones. The young four-year-old wants to go his own way, yet gradually he finds it satisfying to go with others. So he emerges slowly from the self-satisfaction of the "do it myself" attitude to the wider aspect of "let's do it together," or a beginning of group feeling. He does this best when the teacher knows his need for it, lets him take his time, and guides him carefully into happy experiences which provide it.

The four-year-old child is intensely interested in people. He

[2] Ibid., page 1.

likes to recognize "Dick's father" and "Mary's big brother" as they
call at the kindergarten door at closing time. He discovers that the
friendly man he often sees working in the churchyard is the janitor
or sexton. He learns from the adults in his environment the principles of Christianity to the extent to which they practice them. He
senses what the Bible verse, "Be kind," actually means when the
teacher points it out as it occurs in the relationships between these
adults and the child, between children themselves in the midst of
work and play. He sorts out such bits of learning and begins to discover that certain actions cause certain results.

This gay little four-year-old might be compared to the "fluid
drive" which we have in our modern automobiles, in that he shifts
readily from one speed to the next, from one tempo to another, from
one mood, one line of thinking, one activity, to others with rapidity
and smoothness. Smooth, that is, internally, but to the observing
teacher he is quick and almost rough, arms and legs sticking out in
his eagerness and curiosity. It is no wonder that he is this way, for
his big muscles of arms and legs are developing rapidly at this
stage. "Never a still minute" is a literal phrase often used by a
parent to describe a preschool child. Four-year-olds have come a
long way from two and three and can be still for a short while, but it
takes great effort. In fact, one educator puts it this way: "The
hardest thing for them to do is to be inactive. To have to sit still
is more fatiguing than trotting about as they please all morning.
They are more likely to 'get tired sitting still' than to 'get tired.'"[8]
It was perfectly natural for Crystal to say in the housekeeping corner one morning: "I don't want to be the grandma. She just sits
around." To wiggle and twist, to stand, sit, squat—all these shift-
ing positions are part of the growing process.

The four-year-old does not want to be held in, but he gets tired of
freedom all the time. He likes new responsibilities that come his
way, but he wants variety in things to be done. And all the while
what a busy little talker he is! He discovers rather rapidly that
words are an opening into the adult world; he asks questions; he
uses new words he does not understand; he makes up funny words
and phrases; he boasts, to gain an entrance into the wonderful world
of adult attention. "Gosh, you're crazy," said a new child to the
kindergarten teacher. "Miss Esther—fester—dester—mester,"
sang another child and it was laughingly re-echoed by others. Words
of four-year-olds warrant careful thought on the part of the teacher
as to when to ignore, when to laugh, when to question, when to
accept. For the teacher to use only words or questions to find out
what a child has learned is not practical. Often he can express
himself more truly in some other way, such as painting it, playing
it, or making it in clay.

When drawing or painting, a four-year-old will name his picture

[3] *An Introduction to Child Study*, by Ruth Strang, page 158. The Macmillan
Company, 1930.

as he goes along. Blond-haired Bobby was intent in his work. Finally, the teacher stooped down to him where he was painting on the floor and said, "Tell me about your picture, Bobby." He replied: "It's a dead fish. You'll see when I finish." She moved about the room slowly, and later when she neared Bobby, he said in his brash, exultant tones: "It's going to be a big house. No, a ship." At the end of his work he added: "That's the top and that's the bottom. It looks like a tractor."

Both four- and five-year-olds have literal minds and cannot yet comprehend ideas in the lovely symbolic fashion that adults enjoy. If they sing "Jesus wants me for a sunbeam," they think about the actual sunbeam, or they startle us even more by responding as Willard did in terms of modern-day radio advertising. His sister sat listening to the children sing this song on her first Sunday in the kindergarten. She whispered to Willard, age five and a half, "What is a sunbeam?" He replied quickly, "Silly—it's a toaster." Therefore teachers are forced to ask themselves: "Is this actually true as a child is able to interpret it?" The answer is so evident that they do not use that song or any other material with symbolic words. The cross, sin, the "valley of the shadow of death," "Give us this day our daily bread," and many other phrases are to come later when the child is ready to learn them because he can understand them.

There are also other difficulties for kindergarten children in ideas of time, space, and money. For the most part they know what "today" and "yesterday" are, and some children sense the meaning of "tomorrow." We do not stress with them that Jesus was born over two thousand years ago; it is enough that Jesus was born to show that God loves us. A "faraway place" to age four or five may mean the only town where he has been other than that in which he lives and it may be six miles away. They hear of "Bethlehem" and "Palestine" but such places are strange words and not ideas thoroughly grasped. Money also is hard to understand and has meaning to the young child only in terms of his experience. For example, he likes candy, finds out that money buys candy, then money means candy to him. Money if given to him by adults. He does not understand what it means to earn money nor does he comprehend its value or power. Usually he uses it as he is told. Giving money to the church is a habit we wish to start early, but one which has little meaning in kindergarten years. Thus it is important that teachers in the church school make it possible for children to give other kinds of gifts as well as money—things they can make, things that children enjoy using, things they know are needed by all people.

THE FIVE-YEAR-OLD

Five-year-olds begin to have more control of their bodies than four-year-olds in running, skipping, jumping, climbing, and balancing. Though large muscles are still developing, the small muscles of the hands are better controlled than at four, and they can cut quite well with scissors; paste; handle small objects carefully; print their first names; and occasionally tie a bow. In drawing or painting, they plan what they will do, then do it, in contrast to the four-year-old, who names his picture as he goes along. At five the child can draw "a man" that is easily recognized by an adult. He takes pains with his pictures and likes to show them and tell about them, but resents being asked bluntly, "What is it?" "Tell me about your picture" usually gets an enthusiastic response because here is an adult who is interested in his work. He wants to finish his work, even if it is carried over to the next day. He enjoys putting play and work materials away neatly, with other children and teachers all doing it together. He can carry a melody now and his sense of rhythm has developed. The physical structure of his throat makes his singing range from the G above middle C up to E. Dressing every day is done more easily and with less dawdling than when he was four. In kindergarten groups it is not uncommon to see the fives help the fours with aprons, coats, and sweaters. When they play in groups of three or more, they are creative and imaginative in living bits of real life as they know it or see it from the adults in their environment. In playing with blocks, they use figures, dolls, cars, and trucks to make the scene more vivid.

Dr. Gesell says that if not a superman, at least the five-year-old is a "superinfant," careful, polite, and friendly. He is ready for the independence that weekday kindergarten gives him and he accepts it with joy. While mother was once the authority he quoted, he now adds the teacher. In this new adult he does not need a person who will regiment him into a group pattern, lecture to him, boss his every move, but he needs a warm friend who will explore with him, laugh, sing, play, and pray.

The group of children a kindergarten teacher meets in her room have many similarities in their accomplishments according to their ages. But within the physical age limits of four and five there are as many different personalities as there are children. The teacher must expect as much of the small five-year-old as the large and not let physical appearance determine her reactions. Often she will find the small child either shy or aggressive and for good reasons. She must know his age and treat him accordingly. Some fours are ahead of the fives, depending on native ability as evidenced in musical expression; depending on nursery school experience as shown in their ability to get along with other children; depending on parental love as discovered in the lack of fears. Correspondingly, some fives seem more mature in certain areas than some six-year-olds. In other words, while there are basic laws of growth within a certain age span, there are also individual tempos of growth, dependent for the most part upon the child's ability, the type of experience he has had, and the environment in which he has lived up to this point. It can well be repeated: usually it is the <u>adults</u> with whom a child lives who <u>ruin</u> God's wondrous hopes; usually it is the <u>adults</u> with whom a child lives who <u>nurture</u> his holy design.

As teachers of young four- and five-year-olds, we too have a part in the fostering of God's plan for these precious lives. Within us all, old and young alike, is a spark of the divine; we each have the native capacity for religion, for seeking our Creator, but we vary in our approaches to him. And God seeks us, constantly. So the teacher who is attuned to him becomes a channel through which he works to reach a little child. God's laws of growth are constant; the teacher whose children actually learn is using his laws.

<u>DON'T</u>	<u>DO</u>
Dislike a child because he is physically unattractive to you.	Look for the lovable in every child.
Dislike a child because you do not like his parents.	Recognize the aloneness of every human soul.

To the Reader:

Now will you continue the experiment? Take the two lists of your children, and by carefully examining this chapter check the items or things the children do that may be classified as rather typical of this age. You will probably find such things in both lists of children.

Are there any items left on your lists that cause you to ask, "Why is he like this?" Such as: "He is quiet." "He sits still." "He talks only when spoken to." "He hits other children." How are such descriptions reason for a teacher's honest concern for that child? Where can you get help in studying him?

Besides reading the suggested material and books listed, begin to study a child by calling at his home when he is awake, by writing down notations from that visit, by walking in his neighborhood in an effort to see him in his leisure play, by visiting nursery schools or kindergartens, by asking the pastor if he knows the family, by getting an experienced teacher in the church to help you.

READING THAT WILL HELP

Child Development, by Arnold Gesell and Frances Ilg. Harper & Brothers, 1949. $6.00.

Good Education for Young Children. Published by New York State Council for Early Childhood Education.

Some Special Problems of Children, Aged 2 to 5 Years, by Nina Ridenour and Isabel Johnson. New York State Society for Mental Health, Inc., 105 East Twenty-second Street, New York 10, New York. 50 cents.

Understanding Your Child, by James L. Hymes, Jr. Prentice-Hall, Inc., 1952. $2.95.

Your Child from One to Six. Superintendent of Documents, Government Printing Office, Washington 25, D. C. 20 cents.

2. WHAT WE WANT THEM TO LEARN
IN THE CHURCH

Dear Reader:

How do children grow? What fosters or stifles growth? As we teach, how can we be sure that they are learning? How is it possible for a child to learn something the teacher did not intend to teach? What is our purpose in teaching four- and five-year-olds in the church?

Before reading this chapter write briefly your purpose in teaching kindergarten children in the church. What do you hope to achieve? What do you want them to be?

Church school teachers keep their eyes on the mountaintop: that is, they seem to visualize each child as a maturing young person and adult and pray that he will be an active, aggressive disciple of Christ. Teachers must keep their sight on this goal as they pray and work from month to month with young learners. This main goal will keep them in the right direction when they are thinking in terms of one lesson, one Sunday, for one hour. This goal will help teachers to analyze the many parts that go into the making of a maturing Christian disciple. They will realize that a knowledge of the Bible is not sufficient of itself, nor good Christian character, nor concern for others, nor a knowledge of God and Jesus, not even love alone, but a combination of these in a devout heart. They will realize that slowly but surely human growth in the direction of the goal is the way or method of achieving it. The kindergarten teacher's part is to guide the child when he is four and five in experiences with God and Jesus, the Bible and church, himself and others—experiences that will be a part of this major goal, yet at the same time will fit the needs, interests, and capabilities of the children. A kindergarten teacher works with the children only two years, knows that the primary teacher will work three years and the junior three more before many of the children will come to the actual decision to be disciples of Christ. Then other leaders in youth and adulthood help to determine how vital and how active that discipleship will become. The hope of every Christian teacher is that he will do his part well in forwarding this growth, not hindering it.

12

What part of this major goal can be accomplished or worked upon in the kindergarten department?

1. In learning about God, a child can be led:
   a. To thank him in wonder for his beautiful world—the sprouts and flower from a little brown bulb, the scent of the rosy phlox, the colors of a tiny stone, and the clouds of a summer day.
   b. To know from the Bible that God loves him and wants him to learn to help care for himself.
   c. To find God's love in kindly people, usually his parents first, then other adults who are teachers, doctors, neighbors, and older children as well.

2. In learning about Jesus, a child can be led:
   a. To discover that God sent Jesus to tell us of his love.
   b. To realize that Christmas is remembering the time when Jesus came as a baby.
   c. To know that Easter is a time to think about Jesus when he was a man, when he was a strong and loving friend to everyone; and to learn that Jesus is our friend too.
   d. To learn that Jesus always helped people wherever he went.
   e. To find out that Jesus taught people how to live together as God planned for them to live.
   f. To discover that we learn about Jesus in the Bible.

3. In seeing a book called the Bible, a child can be led:
   a. To know that it tells about God and his love.
   b. To know that it tells about Jesus and what he did as he "went about doing good."
   c. To discover that it tells him how to live happily with others in the family, neighborhood, and church.
   d. To realize that it is a very special book, to be read and loved more and more as he grows.

4. In going to the church week by week, a child can be led:
   a. To know that it is a special place where people come to learn about Jesus and God.
   b. To discover that parents bring their babies there to promise God that they will teach them about him and Jesus.
   c. To find out that the church is people who try to help one another as Jesus helped.
   d. To love the church and want to come as often as possible.

5. In growing up, the child himself can be led:
   a. To see that he can learn to do much to care for himself, and that God planned it that way.
   b. To choose what he will do and to learn that grownups want to help him.
   c. To realize that he can do many things to help others, that he is needed.
   d. To find out that the Bible will always help him to know how God wants him to live.

6. In finding his place in a group of children, a child can be led:
   a. To find out that his happiness depends on how well he and the other children work and play together.
   b. To see that taking turns makes him and others happy.
   c. To discover that certain behavior makes for unhappiness and is not to be repeated.
   d. To feel sorry when others are hurt or sick.
   e. To feel sorry and do something to help when others do not have important things like enough food and warm clothing, Bible books, and pictures of Jesus.
   f. To discover that some grownups work to make the neighborhood or city a good place in which to live; to express gratitude to such people as the mailman, milkman, fireman, doctor, and others.
   g. To find out from the Bible that God and Jesus love all kinds of people, wherever they may be, and want them to love each other.

In these detailed purposes of guiding children who are four and five can be seen elements of our major goal of helping them grow toward an intelligent, active, devoted discipleship when they are older.

How do teachers go about accomplishing these things with little children? To tell them about Jesus is not enough. To show them pictures of Jesus is not enough. They must have a feeling of love and warm friendship toward him; they must sense that he is their helper in talking to God in prayer; they must find satisfaction in doing everyday things in his way. In other words, hearing and seeing are not enough, but must be reinforced with doing. When a teacher tells a child something, there is little guarantee that that child learned what was said; when a teacher helps a child to feel, to think, and to do, there is a much wider, stronger guarantee. For it has been proved that a child—yes, and even an adult—remembers or actually learns:

   only 10 per cent of what he hears;
   50 per cent of what he sees;
   and 90 per cent of what he does.

Knowing this, Christian leaders today cannot be satisfied with less than 90 per cent learning as they guide boys and girls and men and women into a mature Christlike life. This seems that the goals or purposes of the church must be translated into experiences for the learners. A teacher does not teach unless a pupil learns. In the past, the church, and secular education as well, has wasted energy through too much telling, which results in only 10 per cent learning.

In looking at four- and five-year-olds, here are some of the ways in which they learn. Look at each item in the left-hand column and notice how the possible learning can be increased in the suggested items of the "Seeing" and "Doing" columns.

HEARING	SEEING	DOING
A story.	A picture of that story. A teacher who imitates the spirit of the story.	Playing the story in part or whole.
A Bible verse.	The Bible and a picture that explains the verse.	Playing the spirit of the verse in a selected situation.
An admonition: 1. You must be kind.	A teacher who is kind to each child, to visitors.	Helping the new child in the room to find a book or toy to use.
2. You must share.	A teacher gives up her chair or cracker for someone else.	Taking a favorite book to a sick friend; taking turns with paint jars, clay, blocks, cars.
3. You must pick up toys and work materials.	A picture of children putting away things; their own teacher actually picking up and putting away with them.	Getting the habit of putting away toys and books and work materials when through using them.
4. You must help mother with baby.	Pictures of people doing different things for babies.	Thinking of ways, telling them, showing how to do them. Bringing mother and baby to visit kindergarten when all the children can do something for the baby.
Music: 1. Instrumental.	Seeing the instrument and the motions of the player, and the sheets of music or hymnal, with their lines and notes.	Skipping, swaying, flying to the rhythms of the music rests muscles and lets out feelings that were pent up within the child. Quiet music helps him to rest.

2. A song.	An object or picture mentioned in the song — such as bird's nest, manger scene, or crèche.	Telling what the song means by story, play, clay, or paint.
<u>A poem read.</u>		Telling how it made the child feel, or what he thought about. Drawing something the poem said to him.
<u>Nature stories and nature Bible verses.</u>	Nature pictures and objects.	Handling stones and leaves, caring for a cocoon or bulb, feeding a pet frog or bird. Talking in wonder about God who made each one. Talking to God in thanking him for them.

Seldom do the items in one column happen alone, for teachers nowadays are not content to do all the talking and just require listening or hearing from their young learners. When all three columns are used in a given item, then the child learns more normally with his whole being in all of these ways.

THREE LAWS OF LEARNING

Teachers have another guide or guarantee of positive results in their work when they know and use rightly the "laws of learning," namely:

1. Law of readiness
2. Law of effect
3. Law of practice or use

These laws can be analyzed in the light of two five-year-olds trying to roller-skate.

<u>The first child:</u>

1. It was springtime and every day Helen saw her big sister and brother whiz down the sidewalk on their roller skates. It looked wonderful; she wanted to try it. Finally she persuaded her mother to let her try. The sister's skates were made smaller and put on Helen.
2. With mother and sister on each side of her, Helen rolled gently along on the ball bearings. They turned faster and faster

so that mother and sister had to run a little. It was a different feeling from any Helen had had before. But she liked it! She wanted to do it all the time. Gradually she learned how to put one foot ahead of the other in gliding fashion. Then only one person helped her by holding her hand, and finally she tried it alone. She took many spills. But the desire to learn to skate was keen.

3. She accepted the hurts and tried some more. Her father bought her a pair of skates so that big sister could use her own, because Helen was trying out this new process every day. She went to her playmate's house on skates. She went on skates to the corner store for a loaf of bread. No matter how hard the tumble and how many the tears, she did not give up. Skating became a real pastime for Helen and she acquired great skill in it as she grew older.

The second child:

1. George got a pair of roller skates for Christmas when he was five because his mother thought it was time he learned since she had learned at his age. His father had grown up in the country and had never learned to roller-skate. His mother coveted for him the fun of roller skating, the thrill of gliding through the air, jumping over cracks in the sidewalk, racing the boys and girls round the block. He was pleased with the gift, for he had seen a few big boys go down the hill on their skates.

2. He tried with one skate and his mother held his arm. It was good. He soon did it alone, even though the foot with the skate often went out of bounds and he sprawled on the sidewalk. Then he got tired and quit. He somehow couldn't sail along on the one skate very often; that foot went out the wrong direction. Other days he would try occasionally and his father and mother helped him.

3. He tried both skates; got along with help, but could hardly walk on them alone. His friends were not skaters; they preferred wagons and "flexies." He knew his father could not skate. Six years later George still could not roller-skate.

Both Helen and George were five-year-olds. Notice that there were reasons for Helen's readiness while in George's case it was his mother who was ready. The pleasure of the experience made Helen want to repeat it; the dissatisfaction George found made him "lukewarm" about roller skating. The achievement of her brother and sister in skating made Helen desire the skill; the lack of interest of his father and friends influenced George against skating. The fact that Helen kept trying and kept skating meant that she learned to be a good skater. The fact that George did not try much even when he was able to walk on the skates meant that he never achieved the skill. Furthermore, and very important in this illustration, is

the fact that Helen and George differed in their physical maturity at
the same age. Helen could skip well even when four; she could cut
on the line with scissors; she could tie a bow, for her muscles
seemed to respond to her desires. To the contrary, George was
somewhat clumsy. He could skip when he was five and a half but
very awkwardly; he could not manipulate a scooter because he could
not balance; he did not learn to tie a bow until he was seven, for
George's muscular co-ordination was slow in maturing. The readiness and lack of readiness in this skating experience for two five-
year-olds was due to their basic physical growth, as well as to their
environment and the people in it. The laws of learning explain why
one child learned and the other child did not learn.

It is important for every teacher to know these laws of learning
and how they operate, so that the teaching done in our churches will
be positive and have lifelong effects. For these laws are noticeable
in every bit of learning. Adults analyze their own experiences and
find them in everyday, common learnings. But when they are consciously used by a teacher with a certain goal, they are manipulated
by the teacher instead of accepted as they naturally occur. That is,
the first law of readiness is conditioned by the teacher, who can, by
careful planning, get boys and girls ready and eager to learn what
she wants to teach them. Then she can guide them into experiences
that are pleasant and happy. Next, she makes it possible for them
to use their newly acquired bit of learning, whether it be an attitude, a feeling, some facts (such as a Bible verse or a song), or the
ability to act in a certain way.

It is readily seen how important these laws of learning are to Sunday church school teachers who see their children only one or two
hours at weekly intervals. The teacher has no time to waste. The
dozen or two dozen children come to the church from as many different kinds of homes: some being brought with care, some being
sent with relief; some fretful from lack of sleep or food; some
insecure with the coming of a new baby at home; some quite secure
with the glow of new shoes. Teachers realize that every Sunday a
group of children arrive as individuals of varying interests and
must be led into being a group sharing the same vital interest.
Teachers also realize that some individuals will learn more than
others on a given day, because of their home background and because their particular need fits into that day's teaching goal. Such a
day for Jimmy would be when he could contribute to the dramatic
play on how a big brother or sister can help mother with the baby
because he has a baby brother at his house. Mature teachers
realize that some children will learn what the teacher has not
planned to teach. For children do learn to be late from a teacher
who is always late; they learn to omit an offering if they never see
the teacher put something into the offering plate; they do not put
their toys away if the teacher does not have a share in doing this.
It is amazing to think that such negative teaching sometimes takes
place in churches! But it is still true that what teachers do speaks

louder than what they say. In the same way, children learn positive things when the teacher is unaware of it; namely, helping a new child get acquainted with everyone because the teacher sets the pattern; putting wastepaper in the wastebasket when seeing the teacher do it; calmly helping wipe up spilled paint when someone has an accident. Bits of learning that were not consciously planned by the teacher are assimilated by children who at four and five years of age are keen to imitate their leaders.

Kindergarten church school teachers must be aware constantly of the laws of growth that God has planned in human beings in order to plan their teaching around the needs, interests, and capabilities of the child at four and five. They must also use the laws of learning as they plan and teach in order to be assured of the best possible growth taking place in their children as individuals and as a group. They must accept these laws of learning for themselves too in teaching themselves new habits and new skills. They must sense that they are not working alone, but are co-workers with God. He moves in the hearts and souls of old and young through the Holy Spirit to help them to seek and to find his will for their daily living. The spirit of the Christian teacher is far more than the drive to tell the children the story of Jesus. The teacher works with God to get the child to know and love Jesus as his best Friend and to want to live the way Jesus taught people to live.

To the Reader:

If you wrote your purpose in teaching kindergarten children in the church before reading this chapter, compare it now with the six elements of the basic goal. Does your purpose include all six? Is it written in terms of "teaching lessons" or of guiding boys and girls in certain Christian experiences?

Analyze your own teaching:

Do you use the laws of learning, all three?
How much do your children do?
How long do your children listen?
Are you willing for them to imitate everything you do?

READING THAT WILL HELP

Guiding Boys and Girls to Christ, by Ralph N. Mould. Board of Christian Education of the Presbyterian Church in the U.S.A. Presbyterian Distribution Service. 30 cents.

Opening the Door for God, by Herman J. Sweet. The Westminster Press, 1944. $1.50.

The Spiritual Growth of Children, by Dorothy B. Fritz. The Westminster Press, 1957. $1.00.

Theology in the New Curriculum. Board of Christian Education of the Presbyterian Church in the U.S.A. 10 cents.

Your Child Grows Toward God, by Pearl Rosser. A pictorial booklet showing stages of religious growth in a child. The Judson Press. 15 cents.

3. A GOOD SUNDAY FOR THESE CHILDREN

Dear Reader:

Perhaps you have often wished you might visit another teacher to see just what she accomplishes in one hour on a Sunday morning. Here is your opportunity! Step into the room where Mrs. Jackson and Mrs. Lewis are at work on a rainy spring morning. As you read jot down questions that you would like to ask them. To find answers to your questions, read carefully the section at the end of the chapter entitled, "Let Us Evaluate This 'Good Sunday,'" which includes do's and don'ts for kindergarten teachers.

"I wonder how many will remember to bring a toy or book today for the children's hospital," said Mrs. Lewis, as she was hanging up her coat and hat in the church kindergarten room on a rainy March Sunday.

"I rather think several will," replied Mrs. Jackson, while she unlocked the supply cabinet. "Mrs. Otto and her parents' committee phoned the homes this week to be sure everyone knew about our special project and about the party tomorrow afternoon. And do you know what? Mrs. Otto offered to bake cookies for the party!"

"Wonderful! How did we get along last year without that parents' committee? They've been the biggest help to us this year."

"Haven't they though! And they're hard at work on the invitations for our evening parents' meeting before Palm Sunday, when Miss Myer is coming to lead the discussion on 'Answering Children's Questions About Life and Death.'"

"The bookstore has promised us that display of books for selling. Did I tell you? And the secretary said that the spring curriculum magazines are already here, so we can give them out as planned. Well, good morning, Tommy. I'm glad to see you."

"Hello, Tommy," said Mrs. Jackson. "We need help. It's good that you are here."

Tommy hung up his coat and hat and went to the cabinet to get out the offering plate and the Bible to put on the little low table. Then he placed his offering envelope in the plate and asked if he could help put up pictures too. He was used to helping because his daddy

20

was a teacher and he often reached the church before the other children. But when John came in, he was off to talk to him and start building with the blocks.

"Look what I have for the sick children! " exclaimed Bill, as he and several others came into the room together. "It's a fire engine. But it's little. You can play with it in bed."

Quiet Nancy walked over to the table to put her offering in the plate, then took her stuffed lamb to the two chairs fixed together to hold the gifts, and back to the coat hooks to hang up her wraps. Mrs. Jackson noticed this and as the children were gathered around the two chairs to look at Bill's fire engine, she mentioned Nancy's lamb and drew Nancy into the group.

"I'd like to have that dog," said Richard. "I like his tail." And he wiggled the spring on a long daschund that someone had brought the week before.

"Someone who is sick in bed will have fun with him, won't he, Richard? " said Mrs. Jackson. The children admired the toys and books, then took off their wraps; other children were being welcomed by Mrs. Lewis, and some were drifting toward the dolls and the table of growing things. As each child brought something, others gathered around him and one of the teachers talked with them about the good times some other children would have who were sick in bed.

At the table of growing things, a little group was noticing how much bigger the sweet-potato roots were this Sunday, and the leaves on the carrot tops.[1] "I have some carrot tops in my house, Mrs. Jackson," said Julie Ann. "My mother cut the carrots off just the way you did and now there are tiny little leaves coming out."

"I have some too," said David, "and they're this high already! "

"The Bible says, 'Stand still, think of the wonders of God.'[2] That is what we are doing when we watch our growing things. That is what this little girl is doing in the picture here on the table easel. What does she think is a wonder of God? "

"A cobweb." "A cobweb with a spider in it." "Yes, and some water is on it too," added David, the one who usually saw the most in pictures.

"There is another wonder of God here that we haven't talked about."

"The brown bulb," said Nicola.

"Say, is that the one we planted! It didn't have any green on it when I was here last," said Evelyn.

---

[1]If a carrot is cut at the top so that there is about one fourth inch of green stems and one fourth inch of yellow carrot, then put in a saucer of water just an eighth or a quarter of an inch deep, it will sprout tiny new leaves which grow four or five inches high. Some children will ask why a whole carrot does not grow, and will have to be helped to understand about seeds, roots, and dirt.
[2]Job 37:14 (Moffatt).

"No, because you have been sick and couldn't be here for a while, Evelyn. We're glad you could come back today to see our amaryllis bulb with green leaves growing. The Bible says, 'Stand still, think of the wonders of God.'" Then Mrs. Jackson began to sing quietly:

> " 'Deep in the earth it is tucked away,
> Brown little bulb that we hide from sight.
> Now it will grow from day to day;
> Soon comes a lily that is tall and bright.' [3]

"Let's sing the song about the bulb."

The father and grandmother, who were sitting in the visitors' chairs, watched with interest. Every child who came was welcomed by one of the teachers, as they themselves had been. Those who needed help with galoshes or coats received it; the others helped themselves in an orderly fashion and some helped one another. Each arrival found a place in the group with Mrs. Jackson or the group with Mrs. Lewis, who was reading at a table near the wallboard for pictures. Some were building with blocks and playing with the dolls in the housekeeping corner. But gradually, with Mrs. Lewis' help, they put away books and toys, except Michael who would not part with the big blue book. Book in hand, he now went happily with the others to stand by the piano and sing the new song about the brown little bulb. Then they sang about the soft rain which God sends to help the bulbs and trees outdoors to grow. [4]

"We could play that we are bulbs sleeping in the ground," said Mrs. Jackson, and she moved away from the piano to the small open space on the rug, pushing back the chairs so that there would be standing room at least for everyone. She stooped down with the children, some of them naming the kind of bulb they would be. Mrs. Jackson and Mrs. Lewis sang the bulb song while they all slept and grew with the words in the song. They played it three times and the children were singing the song too!

Sensing that this bit of rhythm had relaxed the children and united them as a group, Mrs. Jackson invited them to sit down on the rug so that each child could see her and have room without having to crowd anyone else. Looking around at each one, she said: "Evelyn is back today and we are glad she is well again. Ronald is not here because he is visiting his grandmother."

"I won't be here next Sunday," interrupted Jimmy, "because I will be visiting my grandmother. My mommy is going to the hospital to have our baby."

"We'll miss you, but we hope you have a happy time, Jimmy. When you come back and tell us about the new baby at your house, we will all sing for your baby." [5]

---

[3] Adapted from No. 51, in *When the Little Child Wants to Sing*. The Westminster Press, $1.25.

[4] No. 26 in *When the Little Child Wants to Sing*.

[5] No. 99 in *When the Little Child Wants to Sing*.

"My baby's this big now," said Joan stretching out her hands.

Nodding her head in agreement with Joan, Mrs. Jackson then said: "When I look around our room, I see two visitors today. Which children will tell us who they are?"

Susie jumped up and ran over to her daddy, who hugged her. The children smiled and Susie said, "It's my daddy."

"And where is Charles? There you are! Could you point to your grandmother to let us know she is from your house?" Mrs. Jackson welcomed both the grownups.

"Because Evelyn has been absent, she does not know all about our gifts on the chairs. Our visitors do not know either. What are we going to do with these gifts? Bill, would you tell about them?"

A conversation followed about the children in the hospital who need many toys and books, about bringing one from home that we like to play with, and one that can be used in bed.

"Did you see the books I brought? They are about Jesus," said Lee.

"I brought a book. A new one from the store. It is just like the one Aunt Dorothy gave me for my birthday," said Sandra.

"I had to get my gift from the store too," said Mrs. Jackson, "because I do not have toys at my house. I brought a little red car."

"I forgot to bring any," added John.

"There will be one more time to bring things," said the teacher. "Tomorrow afternoon you can bring a toy or book when you come to our room for the party. The man at the grocery store gave me that big box to pack our gifts in. I went to get it just as I promised I would."

Because the children were restless from sitting, Mrs. Jackson stood up and said: " 'I'm sometimes very tall.' Nancy, will you close your eyes and guess what we are?" Then the children stretched their arms up high and stooped low as they said:

> " 'I'm sometimes very tall,
> I'm sometimes very small;
> Sometimes tall,
> Sometimes small,
> Which way am I now?' "[6]

Up and down they went. Donnie had a turn to guess too, then Mrs. Jackson said: "One of our boys is older today. Charles has had a birthday. Let's sing to him.

> " 'Happy birthday we will say,
> For you're five years old today.' "[7]

---

[6] Page 46 in Growing, Vol. I, No. 2.
[7] No. 123 in When the Little Child Wants to Sing.

With her arm around him and a smile, Mrs. Jackson said cheerfully: "Five years old! Charles is five now. He can do more than he could do when he was four. God helped him to grow. Let's thank God for Charles's birthday. 'Dear God, thank you that Charles is five years old. Thank you that he is older now and can do many things to help at home. May he always know that you love and care about him. Amen.'"

"My birthday is next Sunday!"

"Mine is coming soon I know."

"It is time to come together now," said Mrs. Jackson, and the children gathered to one side of the room. Mrs. Lewis and Mrs. Jackson placed the chairs, facing the low table on which Tommy had put the offering plate and the Bible. Over it hung a picture of Jesus and the children. And now the pretty feathery leaves of the carrot added to the table a touch of the growing of springtime.

Mrs. Lewis played the piano while Mrs. Jackson and the children sang their church bell song[8] and leaned over far to pull the rope of the bells, so that the children would stretch and wiggle and be ready to sit still for a while. Then the music changed to "Very softly I will walk"[9] and they walked over to sit on the chairs.

"Every morning of sunshine or snow or rain tells us that God loves us. Let's stand and sing the song[10] that helps us to remember."

"We're glad today too that we could come to church." Mrs. Jackson began to sing the welcome song[11] with the children joining in, then they sat down.

"Every Sunday we bring some money for our offering. Part of the money helps us to have books and pictures in our church. Part of the money helps other children far away to have books and pictures about Jesus. Alfred, will you hold the offering plate today while we sing our offering prayer?" With bowed heads, the children sang, "Father, bless the gifts we bring thee,"[12] and Mrs. Jackson prayed: "Thank you, God, for money to bring to our church. And thank you, God, for the toys and books we can bring to our church. May some sick children be made glad. Amen."

Mrs. Jackson took the open Bible from the table beside her and, turning to the New Testament, she said: "In this part of our Bible there are many stories about a man named Paul. You and I have heard some of them before. Paul went to many towns to tell people about Jesus. One time a letter came to him from faraway friends. It said that they were hungry because there had been no rain, and

---

[8]Page 21 in Growing, Vol. I, No. 1.
[9]No. 8 in When the Little Child Wants to Sing.
[10]No. 15 in When the Little Child Wants to Sing.
[11]No. 57 in When the Little Child Wants to Sing.
[12]No. 65 in When the Little Child Wants to Sing.

all the food—the grain for bread, the fruit, the vegetables—had dried up and could not grow."[13] She held the open Bible while she told the story, and at the close said: "Let us pray. Dear God, thank you that Paul and the other people shared their food with those who did not have enough. Help us to share what we have with others who need it. Amen.

"Just as those people shared food, we are giving our toys and books. Jesus taught us to love and to help each other.

> "'Jesus loves me! Jesus loves you!
> Let's love each other, As He said to do.'"[14]

Mrs. Jackson stood as she started singing the words of the song and the children joined her, and Mrs. Lewis did not play the piano but sang with them.

They then sat down. Mrs. Jackson again took the Bible from the table and opened it at the book of Proverbs. She read: "'Even a child is known by what he does.'[15] When a child shares his books and toys, people know that he is trying to do what Jesus plans for him to do." She reached down back of her chair for some green crepe paper. "There must be some way we could make the big box look pretty to send our gifts to the hospital."

"Put that green paper all around it."

"And paste it on."

"Yes, that would make it look pretty," said Mrs. Jackson. "And if we could make some pictures to put on it, that might be nice too."

"We could draw some pictures with our crayons."

"What could we make?"

"Flowers and trees and birds, because spring is coming."

"Mrs. Lewis will need some helpers to get the paper and crayons. Nancy, Evelyn, and Richard, will you help her? The children sitting near the piano may go to the tables to work. That means Sandra, Michael, Joan, David, Julie Ann, Nicola, Bill, and Jimmy. All the others will work on the floor today."

Soon there was a joyful noise in the kindergarten room as the children chattered and laughed and drew pictures. Mrs. Lewis and Mrs. Jackson moved quietly from one group to another, talking with them about the colors in their pictures, singing softly the song, "Why not share a picture book?"[16] It was a happy room indeed with so many children at work. One by one they finished and looked at each other's pictures, then put away the crayons and papers and put

---

[13]Story, "A New Kind of Letter," p. 44, in <u>Growing</u>, Vol. I, No. 2.
[14]No. 66 in <u>When the Little Child Wants to Sing</u>.
[15]Prov. 20:11 (Moffatt).
[16]No. 64 in <u>When the Little Child Wants to Sing</u>.

on their wraps. At the door Mrs. Jackson said good-by to each one, and reminded them all of the party the next day to pack the gifts for the sick children at the hospital.

When all the children had left, the teachers finished putting away things, straightened the books and chairs. Peter's mother stopped to ask if she could bring some cookies for the party. Then the teachers began talking about the morning's experience.

"Charles's grandmother told me how glad she was to visit today," said Mrs. Lewis. "She says Charles never tells them a thing at home about what he does in church school, and she was surprised that we used the Bible so much and had prayer."

"Children seldom tell about that part anyway," replied Mrs. Jackson. "But they usually do tell about a favorite toy and what they made when they painted. I'm so glad the parents' committee is willing to phone two homes each week and invite them to visit. In our small room we cannot have more than three or four adults visit at one time, and I really think these parents are getting a lot out of it. Wasn't it nice last week when Tommy's mother brought the baby? Oh, Mrs. Lewis, before I forget, I must tell you about Tommy. When I was talking to a little group of children up around the gifts, I asked them this question: 'What do you think the sick children will know about us when they get these gifts?' And Tommy said, 'They'll know that we're loving them.' I was delighted to hear him express it in words."

"Tommy has developed a great deal since he first came into our room when he was four. Now he is almost six. It's wonderful to see children grow from one stage into another. What about our opening work period today, and the fellowship period? How can we improve next Sunday?"

The two teachers spoke briefly about the morning's experience, and arranged to phone each other on Tuesday with written ideas and plans for the next Sunday. Then they left for the sanctuary and morning worship, reminding each other to come back to the room afterward to take home the growing things so they would be warm and watered all week, and to get the names of absentees to phone them about the next day's party.

LET US EVALUATE THIS "GOOD SUNDAY"

This experience with Mrs. Jackson, Mrs. Lewis, and their children took place in a one-hour Sunday church school session. It was longer for some, because the teachers were there a half hour early so that early comers benefited from more than an hour in their church. There were twenty-three children present, in a room too small for that number. With only two small tables, the children were used to working on the floor. Notice that the tables and chairs were used in a flexible way and moved about. The two visitors' chairs were in one corner out of the line of traffic. A beautiful rug had been given to the room by a grandmother who moved to a smaller house and knew of the need through her daughter who was on the parents' committee. Sitting on the rug was a happy, intimate time for friends old and young. A cabinet held the materials during the week to protect them from dust. The books were kept in an orange crate, painted light green to match the chairs.

Here are some things we might learn from Mrs. Jackson and Mrs. Lewis:

DON'T	DO
Reach the kindergarten room after children arrive.	Come early and remove wraps.
Make the plans for the day after you get there.	Work together as teachers, plan ahead, know your purpose for each session.
Teach children that giving is easy, giving "what you do not want."	Teach children to give because they want to make someone happy.
Overlook the quiet child.	Recognize a Nancy and her gift.
Ask too much of a quiet child.	Let a child make the easy introduction by pointing.
Ask for review.	Use a returned absentee or visitor as an opportunity for thinking again about what the group is doing and why.
Talk about everything mentioned by children.	Acknowledge the child by a nod of the head or a smile.
Use an unappetizing wooden birthday cake.	Stress the joy of growing and learning to do more. Show that God is in birthdays.
Practice songs or poems line by line.	Use them many, many times with individuals and the group.
Require children to "sit still" or to sit for a long time. (See Chapter 1 again.)	Watch them and use dramatic play, a game, or a rhythm; alternate standing and sitting in brief periods.
Use the same routine all the year.	Vary the routine. For example, the church bell song was a carry-over from the previous unit and not used every Sunday.

DON'T	DO
Say: "Wouldn't you like to sing a song? What one shall we sing?" when trying to lead a group with the purpose of worship. (See Chapter 4, page 34, describing worship in playtime, and page 43 entitled "Worship.")	Say: "Let's sing----------," or just begin singing.
Wait for pianist to find page.	Just begin singing—the piano is not always necessary.
Pray long.	Use short prayers with meaningful words.
Insist on folding hands, closing eyes, bowing heads, with feet flat on the floor as the position for praying.	Remember that we really want children to discover that they can talk to God any time, anywhere, in any position, and that they learn by doing.
Always tell the children exactly what to do.	Let the power of suggestion work — as Mrs. Jackson's green paper. If she had not had it, they might have suggested another color, or have wanted to paint the box, which would have been all right. Help them to think for themselves, as they did the next day when they actually put the paper on the box.
Take valuable time to call every name and mark attendance.	Save time for more important matters. For example, Mrs. Lewis marked the attendance record while Mrs. Jackson led the children in conversation.
Let the treasurer come in for the money. (Does it absolutely have to be counted before church?)	Avoid interruptions. Hand offering to the treasurer at the close.
Leave the room without exchanging reactions with the teachers	Write down comments made by the children which will help you in keeping a growing record of them, or in knowing why you absolutely must call in a certain home that week.

DON'T	DO
	(For two Sundays before this Michael had been adamant in hanging on to a book. The teacher found out why and let it be a passing fancy.)
	Plan with the teachers how to avoid some mistakes, how to rearrange the room, what to carry over to completion the next time.
Put messy activities like painting on the impossible list.	Use it on a weekday. These children brought aprons the next day and painted something about the springtime story they were told.
Feel that children expect elaborate refreshments.	Have simple but attractive refreshments, as cookies in cutout shapes.
Think that a party has to be only games and food.	Tell stories, sing, pray, paint, use clay, play games, and have a rhythm band. Make a party a happy, normal experience for children in the church in keeping with your Christian purpose for them.

4. WAYS OF GUIDING CHILDREN
IN CHRISTIAN GROWTH

Dear Reader:

If you are just beginning to teach kindergarten children, you will want to look at the list below to see some of the possible ways you can use to help them learn.

If you are already a kindergarten teacher, what do you do to improve your teaching? How many ways do you use to help them learn? Have you done any observing of a good kindergarten teacher to help yourself improve in the use of these techniques? On the following list, check the ways you used last Sunday. Then double check the ways you have never or seldom used.

> Play—in several ways
> Creative activities and excursions:
>> painting with brushes
>> finger painting
>> clay work
> Music:
>> listening as well as singing
> Conversation
>> and how to ask good questions
> Storytelling
> Using the Bible
> Worship and prayer
> Appreciation
> Rest

In the day-by-day growing of little children Godward, the home is supremely important, for it is there that the preschool child learns the most about life and the world around him. In our curriculum magazines for parents and teachers, special articles are directed toward helping parents in this their high calling. The limited space in this booklet forces us to consider here only those ways of approach that concern us as teachers in the church.

PLAY

Play is the most natural way a child has of learning, of growing. Play to him is work—hard work. To the adult, play is leisure and relaxation, and oftentimes teachers do not understand that play is God's plan for the child's normal growing. A child plays what he sees about him. Adult life is highly desirable to him, so he plays house and tells the doll children what they can or cannot do; he plays doctor and bandages the sick; he plays carpenter and builds a big factory with blocks. In this play, adult life becomes real and he has an active part in it, instead of just watching as in real life.

Photograph by The Van Trotts

Play is essential to the child: it is an outlet for him; it can help him to get rid of some feelings now which may make the way clear for him to be more content and secure, today as well as in the future. So, in a way, play can be medicine for a little child as well as work, for it has a healing quality. This kind of play is usually the kind that adults do not like: it is pounding the clay vigorously; it is knocking down his own blocks; it is running with abandon.

Teachers in church schools who have learned that play is the child's best way of learning and working are including it in the Sunday morning hour. Teachers who have learned that words are too new to four- and five-year-olds for them to grasp their meaning and use them aright are talking less to them about "the lesson for today is. . ." and are including directed play in the Sunday morning hour.

In the church school, play may be used:
1. With toys informally. Dolls, doll clothes and furniture, a broom,

a handbag, and dishes make for many experiences in homemaking. We can say, "God plans for a baby to have a father and mother to take care of it," but when we see and hear young children playing house, we realize that good parents are already in the making. Big blocks, cars, trucks, and some stand-up figures of people in another corner of the room invite young builders and mechanics, and also little Sue, who is proud that her father works in the soybean factory so she built a factory with a huge round smokestack. Here many children learn that they cannot have all the blocks they want; that they cannot knock down what another child has built unless permission from the child is given. Here many children learn to work together in a co-operative way when several make one building, planning and working, taking down and making better, admiring and asking others to "come see." Kindergarten boys and girls are interested in simple puzzles too, and will work a long time to find the way to fit together the pieces into a colorful picture. Playtime that is informal in small groups around the room offers to the child an opportunity to choose what he will do, to get acquainted with others like himself, and to find out how to live with them.

2. In simple games. A game unites a group of varied interests into one, gives rest to tired muscles by allowing them to move as they please, and gives group pleasure or displeasure, which is basic learning for life. In the description of "a good Sunday" in Chapter 3, notice how Mrs. Jackson used a suitable game. Some games help children (and teachers too in a large group!) to know

the names of each child, because the name has to be called as the ball is rolled, or as turns are taken. Many times a game is the way to get acquainted with an adult visitor such as the minister or sexton. Before a group of children went into the sanctuary to see and hear the big organ played, they got acquainted with the organist in their own room. They laughed with delight when with a smile and no hesitation he sat down on the floor and entered into their simple ball game. They were quickly friends, while before this he had been a mysterious man called "the organist."

3. As dramatic play, or, "this is how to do it." The word "acting" is the adult word for this kind of play, but for kindergartners it is simply doing something to express how they feel. The teacher uses it to help a child to understand a Bible verse, such as, "What can you do to show us what 'Be gentle towards all'[1] means? Let's pretend that this doll is my baby. How would you hold the baby? Come and show us." "If the baby dropped his rattle, what might you do? Will you show us?" "If the baby cried, how could you help?"

Dramatic play can be done by a group too, as when they "tiptoe very softly" to see the baby Jesus asleep on the hay while the teacher sings the song "A Christmas Carol."[2] One group of children followed the teacher closely when she told the well-loved story of Jesus' blessing the children. She asked questions about how this father in the picture might have felt, and this little boy. She asked if they would like to pretend that they were going to see Jesus. They walked up to the picture of him smiling under the pomegranate tree[3] in such a way that the teacher felt they loved him dearly, and she silently thanked God for the moment of worship she felt they had had together.

In dramatic play, then, the child can live the story he has just heard; he can explain what he understands about a Bible verse, a song, or a poem. Sometimes misunderstandings are corrected. But play means more than words can mean to fours and fives, and is a natural way of expression.

One summer morning in a vacation school, a teacher used informal toy play and connected it with dramatic play to fulfill her purpose for the morning. The block builders had made a road that morning; it was about twenty feet long and of single, wide, flat blocks. It was "a road to New York" for these San Francisco children. It drew the interest of all the children in the room. So they all went to New York, and, when they got there, sat down on the floor. Here they were right beside a wallboard with a group of pictures showing children helping others in various situations. They talked about each picture, and when they came

---

[1] II Timothy 2:24 (A.S.V.).

[2] No. 39 in When the Little Child Wants to Sing.

[3] A picture entitled, Of Such Is the Kingdom of Heaven, by Elsie Anna Wood.

to the one showing a little girl taking a flower to a sick lady sitting with a blue blanket over her knees, the teacher began to tell a story. At the close, she asked if they would like to play the story. Mary wanted to be the sick lady and Carol suggested that she use the teacher's blue sweater for the blanket over her knees. Lowell, who always thought fast, reached for the flowers on the nearby table to carry to the sick lady. The others felt dismayed until the teacher asked, "What else would a sick lady enjoy?" Books, crayons, a puzzle, and Lowell's bouquet, divided among several children, were soon ready to take. So they all traveled a long way, walking carefully on the block road to make a sick lady happy. Several had thought of interesting things to say to the lady, while others just handed her their gifts. The teacher said that perhaps the sick lady would like to hear them sing, so they sang two songs that the children suggested.

> The teacher said: " 'I like to think of Jesus
> So loving, kind and true
> That somehow when I think of him
> It makes me loving, too.' "[4]

She began to sing and the children joined her:

> " 'Jesus loves me! Jesus loves you!
> Let's love each other, As he said to do.' "[5]

She picked up her Bible and read: " 'Jesus . . . went about doing good, . . . for God was with him.' " Then she said: "One good thing that Jesus did was to help sick people. One day he was at the home of his friend Peter," and she told the story of Jesus healing Peter's wife's mother. She thanked God for Jesus, who helped sick people; they sang again the song they had just sung before the story; and she said, "Children can show that they love Jesus by helping sick people." "By taking them flowers," "and books," "and singing songs to them," responded the children from their dramatic play. Cleanup time was easy now; the road had been used and appreciated.

4. As rhythms for relaxation and rest. After a work or listening period, four- and five-year-olds are ready to wiggle and stretch and move about. They find joy in music that speaks to them of skipping, or walking, or flying. They find pleasure and rest in a kind of "follow the leader" rhythm, when the teacher sings words that suggest action and they follow her in doing it. It can be done even in a rather crowded space, and children learn

---

[4] Elizabeth McE. Shields. Copyright, 1935, by the Presbyterian Board of Christian Education.
[5] No. 66 in When the Little Child Wants to Sing.

something about playing together in this way too, besides stretching those little bodies that need to twist and turn.

CREATIVE ACTIVITIES

The activity of little children, the work that they do with their hands and minds, must have a purpose related to the rest of the hour. It is not sufficient to say, "Today we'll draw, or paint." For the work they do is important in the learning we want to take place. Chapter 2 emphasizes the need for children to learn through doing, and suggests several ways in the "Doing" columns. The important part of this doing in the teacher's mind as she plans is the four basic steps of a satisfying and complete experience for the group. Namely:

1. The decision to do a certain thing.
2. Making plans as to how to do it.
3. The actual doing of those plans by the group.
4. Taking time afterward to evaluate the work the group did.

The key word in each step is "group." Too many teachers are guilty of substituting "the teacher" in these steps. It is true that the teacher may decide to have the children do so-and-so, <u>but</u> it is important that she lead them to decide for themselves. The plans they suggest may be different from those she had in mind; sometimes children's plans are better than their teachers'; sometimes the teacher needs to help the children to think through to a better way of doing. When the children do the work, the teacher does not need to have her hands on their brushes or her fingers in the paste, else it becomes her work instead of theirs! But she does need to be there to answer questions, to ask questions, to make comments that promote the ongoing work. In the description of "a good Sunday" in Chapter 3, you notice how Mrs. Jackson led the children into making their packing box attractive. At the party, as soon as they came, they cut out the pictures they had drawn on Sunday; then they pasted the green paper on the box, bending it down over the top. Mrs. Jackson only held on to the heavy end of crepe paper not yet in place. They pasted the pictures on the box, packed it, then admired their work. Complete evaluation came the next Sunday when the teacher read this letter from the recreational therapist who received the gifts.

"Dear Children:

"The Easter box you made for our children at the hospital certainly was nice. Everything you boys and girls collected is something that our patients like to use.

"I took the box up to second floor and the boys and girls had a grand time looking at the things. The toys and books are two things our children always enjoy looking at and playing with during their time at the hospital.

"The box was decorated so nicely that the boys are keeping it in the ward for a toy box.

"Thank you so much for remembering our children.

> "Barbara Brown,
> "Recreational Therapist."

The entire project, from the first story about children in the hospital who needed many things to keep them happy, was carried through four Sundays (including the last when the letter was read), using the four basic steps necessary for good learning.

At the same time, these children were having springtime experiences before Easter. The bulb they so carefully tended had big buds for Easter Day and two beautiful amaryllis blossoms on the Sunday afterward, when they decided to take it to an elderly lady who could not get out of her house. Richard and Sandra took the plant and had a good time with the lady and her yellow canary; then they told the other children about it the next Sunday.

A consecrated teacher who is truly eager for her children to learn how to love as God wants people to love will never be satisfied to use isolated work periods of coloring, cutting, and pasting. She will study her curriculum materials and use her creative energies to discover interesting work to be done. She will also watch the children and listen to their comments for such discoveries.

Some interesting things to do are:

1. Illustrate a song by drawing or painting pictures of some part of it, evaluating them, pasting them on a long strip of wrapping or wallpaper to hang on the wall, and using them as a help in learning the entire song. "Why not share a picture book? " and "What does the robin say? " are both suitable for this.[6]
2. Use clay, first for the feel of it and the fun of it if the children are not used to it, then for making a gift for someone at home at Christmas time, such as a pencil holder or paperweight. Shapes can vary, but if it is to hold a pencil, it must have a hole in it made by a pencil when the clay was soft. Poster paints and shellac finish the gift when the clay is hard; or, instead, a colored enamel can be used. Figures for a manger scene are interesting work with clay; also an imprint of the child's hand in a large, flat piece of clay.
3. Paint, with brushes, using poster paint on large sheets (18" x 24") of paper. Working on the floor is easy for children. Six

---

[6]Nos. 64 and 21 in When the Little Child Wants to Sing.

can work on a large sheet of oilcloth, with the jars of paint between their papers in the middle. Taking turns is a large part of this work.

Photograph by Rod Williams

Finger painting is excellent, and perhaps the choice work with hands for preschool children. In a vacation church school, Janet had learned to paint with a brush and had seemed happy in her work. One morning the teacher had finger paint ready too and let the children choose which they wanted to do. Janet chose the finger painting. The teacher watched the children silently, after giving brief instructions on how to use it (use wet paper with a spoonful of paint. By spreading the paint all over to the edges, make different marks as your fingers or arms wish to do). It was evident in her expression and manner that Janet had "let go." She was completely satisfied in this new and messy experience. After a while the teacher said to her softly, "Which kind of painting do you like better, Janet?" "This kind. Much better than that," and she made a gesture toward Phyllis who was busy on the floor with brush painting.

In finger painting, fingers do not need to manipulate a tool; the fingers, hands, arms, and elbows do the work. Glazed shelf paper is acceptable or the paper made especially for finger painting. Finger paint is easily made in quantities for a group:

1½ cup laundry starch mixed with enough cold water to make a paste. Add
1 quart boiling water and cook until mixture is transparent or clear. Stir continuously and add
½ cup talcum (can be omitted since it is used only for fragrance). Let cool, and add
1½ cup soap flakes, mixing well until thoroughly blended. Let cool and pour into 8 jars with screw tops. Stir into each jar sufficient poster or powder paint to make desired color.

While this paint is not practical in most churches on Sundays, it is delightful in vacation church schools and at weekday parties. Some kindergarten children (during a unit on "Our Church") made a large church out of a mattress carton. The windows were finger paintings which showed the beautiful colors of the stained-glass windows in their real church as they had seen them when the sun shone through. This activity, involving much deciding, planning, doing, and evaluating, was done in a kindergarten department that has a two-and-a-half-hour session on Sunday mornings. They keep their own aprons (or daddies' shirts worn backward for a smock) at the church to wear when they paint.

4. Paste pictures on cards to mail to children who are absent; pictures on a poster that tell about one idea such as how to help baby, God's gifts of food, etc. In a unit on friends the children can draw their own houses, cut, paste onto a long piece of paper, draw trees and flowers, put on a church, sing "Our street's a friendly street," answer the door in dramatic play when the teacher goes along the street to visit.

MUSIC

Music is a basic need in the religious nurture of growing children. It is vital even in the one-room church where a teacher meets four or six kindergarten children in a corner. She does not need a piano to have music; she does not need a phonograph to have music. If she can sing simply and sweetly, she can guide her children in many ways through music. Churches that can devote a separate room to each department can make good use of an instrument. But a singing teacher is a joy to little children. Music may well be used:

1. In listening. An instrument or a voice can provide through music an atmosphere that bespeaks to the children rest, or fun, or worship. On a hot June day in vacation church school it is important for the child to rest, and well-chosen music helps him to relax and be content. Other music invites him to skip and run, to hop

and glide. The humming or singing of the teacher can lead the children into feelings of reverence in connection with the experience they are having. "Silent Night," played on the phonograph as the children entered their room one Christmas Sunday, changed their thoughts from the world outside to the beauty and joy of the church.

2. In singing. Kindergarten children readily join a singing teacher, and through her spirit and repetition acquire the song for their own. If a piano is used, the melody alone is enough for guidance, and later only a simple harmony. If no piano is used, the leader must be certain to pitch the songs high, within the range between G (above middle C) and the E or E flat above. She must let the children sing sweetly, not asking for the singing to be louder. She must be aware of an original song that is sung spontaneously as a child is at work or play, and acknowledge it and use it. She must be quick to sing a song that suggests the conduct desired when she would help some children in difficulty to straighten out their actions. Sometimes she can use as a song-story a song that is too long for the children to learn. After the story of Jesus and the children, a teacher sang softly, "Children came one summer's day to a Friend."[7] Sometimes a mother is invited to visit and be ready to sing a song-story. Questions afterward help to discover whether or not the children got the meanings clearly.

3. As rhythms for rest and relaxation. This was referred to earlier in this chapter under "Play." For the enjoyment of music, here may be added the use of simple rhythm instruments, such as sticks, bells, and sandpaper-covered blocks.

Often in cleanup time when the group is restless and not working together well, the teacher can quietly recognize with them that they are tired and need to rest before finishing. She may suggest that they sit down right where they are for a little while as she sings or plays a restful melody.

CONVERSATION

Communication between people is usually through the give-and-take of words. While words are new to little children, they enjoy using them, and often make excuses to have a little conversation with an adult, the most noticeable of which is asking questions. Individual attention as the children arrive is important for this give-and-take of personalities. If a teacher will listen more than she speaks, she will find that a few questions can open a child's mind and heart to expressing many of his joys and problems.

Stimulating conversation in play and work groups develops the

---

[7] No. 47 in When the Little Child Wants to Sing.

beginnings of group thinking. But a teacher must study the art of asking questions. Too frequently her questions cause her trouble and lead the children off to unrelated subjects. Sometimes, because the question can be answered easily by "Yes" or "No," that question ends the group thinking. Then again at the right place it may unite the group. A teacher can work on the wording of questions ahead of time when the questions follow the story she will tell. In the questions she will want to find out if the children got the correct ideas from it, so she will be able to plan in advance. This work helps her to develop ability in asking spontaneous questions: Who, What, When, Where, and Why? For example: after the story of Jesus and the children,

DON'T ASK	DO ASK
Did the children like Jesus?	Why did the children love Jesus?
Did he tell the grownups to let the children come close to him?	What did he say?

Many children do not use their minds in church school because not enough is required of them. Let us help them by asking questions that will make them think.

Conversation comes in and out of a session with little children and, like the cord that holds beads together, is the connecting link between play, singing, painting, and cleaning up, etc. It is an important art for a teacher to develop through reading, study, work, and use.

STORIES

Persons of every age are moved by a good story told beautifully. But published stories are not good stories for children. When selecting a story to use with children, ask this about it:

1. Is it a good story in structure?
   Simple plot, with a brief introduction, action moving to a climax, short conclusion.
   Clear sentences, picturesque words, conversation, rhythm, and repetition.
2. Does it suit four- and five-year-olds?
   Vocabulary within their understanding.
   Ideas within their understanding.
   Short in length, especially for group use.
   Teachers find help in analyzing stories for four- and five-year-olds by reading Mitchell's Another Here and Now Story Book.
3. Does it fulfill the teaching purpose?
   Is it consistent with your Christian beliefs? That is, does it

help develop the purpose of your session, and is it in line with Christian attitudes? Some stories written for children make fun of other people, suggest wrong conduct, prey too heavily upon emotions.

4. Do you like it? Do you delight in it?
   If so, when you tell it, the story will be more than words from a printed page; you will give yourself in the telling.
   Many good stories are not effective because they are told poorly or read in an uninteresting manner. In all our work with little children let us remember that they are absorbing something from us—the tone of our voices, the look in our eyes. Let us possess the good story through studying it all week. One teacher does it this way:
   a. Reads the story, or stories, on Sunday afternoon for the next Sunday.
   b. Reads it once every day, preferably first thing in the morning or last thing at night.
   c. Tries to tell it on Friday.
   d. Tells it again on Saturday, asking herself: Do I tell it so that my children will see it, feel it, and sometimes even taste it and smell it?

USING THE BIBLE

There are two ways of using the Bible with children: first, to give them facts from it; second, to develop in them certain attitudes toward it. Both ways are important, but in the kindergarten stage of growing, much emphasis should be placed on attitudes. Only certain stories and verses are within the everyday living and understanding of four- and five-year-olds. These two years of their lives are a slim bit of childhood, youth, and adulthood. These two years of limited mental capacities are more important therefore as a time for parents and teachers to develop in the child desire, eagerness, curiosity, love, and reverence for the Bible. These are basic to his needs if he would seek to know what God says to him through the Bible as he grows.

When in kindergarten, a child is fortunate who sees his parents reading the Bible in his home and hears them talk about it from day to day. He finds also that this Bible is a special book in his church room. It really is important because it tells about God and Jesus and how children and grownups can live together happily.

A devout mother hesitatingly confided to the kindergarten teacher one day that her son was resisting Bible stories and expressing dislike for them. She felt bad, for she had tried sincerely to help him know the Bible. The teacher lent her a book entitled Opening the Bible to Children, by Elizabeth S. Whitehouse. After reading it, the mother said to the teacher: "I see my mistake. I was using stories and passages too old for him; he couldn't understand them.

But I was so anxious to have him get a good start in knowing the Bible. Now he won't listen; he says he hates it. What shall I do?" The sympathetic teacher suggested that she and her husband read it silently, and with some comment to each other, in the presence of the child; that their Bibles be on the breakfast room table or bedside table where the child could see that they were often used and needed and loved.

DON'T	DO
Recognize the Bible only because it is a best seller.	Accept its authority for your own living.
Think of the Bible as subject matter only.	Use it for lifting and inspiring your own spirit.
Accept only one version.	Study several versions and know why they were made.
	Use that version with kindergarten children which is best understood in their language.
Have a superstitious attitude toward the Bible.	Underline favorite verses. Write comments in the margins.
	Black is not the only color used for its covers. Beautiful Bibles are bound in red and in blue leather.
Be afraid to use an everyday story with a Bible verse.	Sense that everyday examples help to interpret Bible teachings.
Think that a child has learned the spirit of a verse because he can say it from memory.	Let the children use dramatic play to show what the verse means.
	Let them make up a song using the verse, or find one in the kindergarten songbooks.
	Use pictures to interpret Bible stories and verses.
	Say a verse aloud many times as it fits the work and play being done.
Read the Bible passage out of the teacher's magazine.	Read from the Bible, beautifully.

Teachers in primary departments have often said that when the first-grade children come into their room they can tell which ones have come from kindergartens where the Bible was used carefully and intelligently. They are the children who, because of desire and love, are eager to learn more from the Bible in keeping with their maturing mental capacities.

WORSHIP

Guiding young children in worship is an art that requires careful thought and practice. Singing and praying together gives group experiences to the five-year-olds and stimulates their thinking and feeling toward God. Yet a teacher cannot be unaware of the four-year-olds, who are still quite individualistic. A long or quite formal worship period is meaningless to children of kindergarten age. Much of their worship will come rather spontaneously (with guidance) in connection with various experiences during the hour's session. Spontaneous worship at the table of growing things may have meant more to that little group in Mrs. Jackson's room than the offering prayer. The prayer for Charles's birthday may have been a time for others to feel God near.

Whether or not true worship takes place depends upon the leader in such a situation, her attitude, her manner, her blending of songs, story, picture, prayer, offering, quiet music. In a crowded kindergarten room, such as many churches have these days, it takes a sensitive, alert teacher to capture the moments that may make for meaningful prayer. For one group which is arranging flowers, talking about their colors, their fragrance, their beauty, God the Maker is very near, and it is natural to thank him for what they have discovered. To another group, building a church of big blocks, with Etola putting in partitions and pointing out rooms for big people and little people, singing together "Our Dear Church Was Builded"[8] led naturally to thanking God for their church.

To lead kindergartners in worship means that first the teacher much know how to worship as an individual, and then she must understand the needs and capacities of the children, letting the expression of worship be brief at the moment of togetherness.

APPRECIATION

Taking time to look at a beautiful stone or a tiny orange beetle, or to smell the fresh lilacs of spring, or to taste the cooky or cracker at lunch time, or to hear the sound of the wind or the soft patter of rain—taking time is important for children. When we stop to watch them, we find them naturally taking time for little things; it is the adult who is apt to hurry by with the rush of many things to be done. Too much talking and too much hurry are not

---

[8]No. 1 in When the Little Child Wants to Sing.

conducive to appreciation. Quietly looking at a lovely picture, listening to beautiful music, hearing over and over again a loved Bible story, feeling the gladness of being together—all these are what it means to take time to appreciate.

New situations and people are met in pictures also. Something of the child's relationship to these situations and persons is felt and his thinking is developed. The beginnings of knowing that this is truly one world with one Father find their lodging in the child's heart quite often through pictures of other children, through dolls of other skin color and hair style.

A teacher selected four pictures from the book Small Rain, by Elizabeth Orton Jones, and used Kodachrome slides to project them on the plain wall of her kindergarten room one vacation morning. There was time to look at each picture when the images of the children appearing on the wall were lifesize. The teacher commented briefly on each, waited, listened to the children's comments, sang a song that fitted one of the pictures. The last picture was the one of a child holding a book. The teacher held her Bible with the red leather covers and commented on how she loved it and how children could love it too. Janet moved from her place on the floor and walked to the wall to feel, to see if the child and the book were real. It was a good illustration of how a competent, loving teacher can help children to appreciate the beautiful.

Pictures, music, poetry, stories, nature, people, are all things to appreciate, as well as the child's own body and the things it can do. Love comes close to appreciation, and love of God and Jesus follow close upon the child's appreciation of lovely things and people.

REST

In a one-hour session on Sunday morning, a rest period of lying down on mats is not as necessary as it is in a longer session and in vacation school. But rest is necessary, in that the elements of the morning move from active to inactive periods rather frequently. As noted in Chapter 1, children of this age "get tired sitting still," and the leader must be aware of this and make provision for moving about, as Mrs. Jackson did in the Sunday morning described. Children get tired, too, from being pushed from one thing to another, without time to enjoy any one item. Children get tired from excessive talking by the adult leader. Wise teachers evaluate each hour they spend with children in an effort to provide needed rest in various ways.

SOME DO'S AND DON'TS

After reading these first four chapters let us consider some important Do's and Don'ts for teachers of four- and five-year-olds. Let us remember that they are growing according to God's laws. Certain characteristics and capabilities predominate as well as certain limitations because of their age and stage of growth.

<ins>DON'T</ins>	<ins>DO</ins>
Ask the children to sit in a circle and wait for church school to begin.	Be ready early. Provide the kind of room or corner that has interesting things for a child to do informally when he first arrives. (See Chapter 5.)
Rush up to a child to take off his coat and hat.	Co-operate with the parents in encouraging self-help. Praise the child for the part he can do by himself, and help him at the hard points, such as hooks on galoshes, coat button under chin, snaps that are too firm for small fingers, snowsuits with crossed straps behind.
Require a four- and five-year-old to sit still.	Let children wiggle when sitting for a story, conversation, and songs. If they get too restless, let them stand, move to another part of the room, have dramatic play.
Tell the children what to do in great detail.	Encourage them to think and use their imaginations.
Demand long periods of silence.	Let them make comments to each other as they work and play.
Let them talk to each other during the prayers.	Make the prayers short, with no other talking.
Talk too much, and on and on.	Let children work and think and play without the constant talking of an adult nearby.
Talk to the other teachers while children are busy.	Use this time to observe the individual children carefully and listen to their conversations with each other.
Talk only to the group.	Hold individual conversations with children at informal times.
Think that every session should follow the same pattern.	Have some pattern of routine, but also some variety within it.

DON'T	DO
Think that books are the only source of learning.	Remember that the child's best tools for learning are his senses. Use things he can see, hear, feel, smell, and taste!
Forget that people who visit can be a real source of information and pleasure.	Plan for visitors of different kinds and for different purposes. A mother to sing a song-story, a teacher who is Japanese, a doctor, the church sexton.
Think that all your teaching must take place on Sunday morning or in the church.	Have weekday excursions—to visit the minister, to help the sick, to see or feel something interesting, to have a party, to enjoy the outdoors.
Look upon the group as a group only.	See each child as an individual within the group and think of him as you plan and teach.
Accept parrotlike answers to questions.	Think whether or not the child has given you an answer in your words or his. Ask more questions, but, better still, find out if he has the right learning of it by letting him paint, or draw, or act out his answer.
Try to review last Sunday's work by questioning.	Keep using stories, pictures, and Bible verses, for repetition is good teaching.

To the Reader:

If you have not observed a trained kindergarten teacher, try to do so. Visit the public schools in your community and see as many rooms and teachers as possible. Attend a Laboratory School in the summertime, where you watch and study for two weeks under guidance. (For information, write to Department of Children's Program, 1105 Witherspoon Building, Philadelphia 7, Pennsylvania.) Teachers are never too old or too experienced to learn, and wise teachers keep seeking help.

FOR YOUR READING

How to
Teach

Guiding Kindergarten Children in the Church School, by Elizabeth McE. Shields. Revised by Dorothea G. Mallard. John Knox Press, 1955, $2.00.

Play and
Learning

These Are Your Children, by Gladys G. Jenkins, Helen Shacter, and William W. Bauer. Scott, Foresman and Company, 1949. $2.50.

Play as Medicine!	A Pound of Prevention, by James L. Hymes, Jr. New York State Committee on Mental Hygiene, 1947.
What to Do and When to Do It Where to Get and How to Use	Religion in the Kindergarten, by Rosemary K. Roorbach. Harper & Brothers, 1949. $2.00. Portfolio for Kindergarten Teachers. Association for Childhood Education International, 1200 Fifteenth Street, N.W., Washington 5, D.C. 75 cents. Portfolio on Materials for Work and Play. Association for Childhood Education International, 1200 Fifteenth Street, N.W., Washington 5, D.C. 75 cents.

5. A PLACE CHILDREN CAN CALL THEIR OWN

Dear Reader:

Have you ever stopped to realize what a room does to your adult feelings? A cozy book-lined room with an easy chair invites you to enjoy books; a shining kitchen invites you to experiment with a recipe; a beautiful church sanctuary impels you to worship; a church room of busy sewing machines enlists your interest in sewing.
Think of other places and what they do to your thoughts. Some repel; some invite. In some you conform; in some you create. Because of some you are bored; because of others you are glad and content. Places do the same to little children! What does the place for four- and five-year-olds in your church do to them?

The time is passing or gone in most churches when the children are given the dark basement room while the adults use "the parlor." The time is also passing or gone in most churches when preschool children are required to meet in big pews with young people and adults. For little children need a place they can call their own. They need a corner screened off from grownups, with their own belongings within reach; or a large sunny room fixed especially for them. Here they will say, "My church."
There are two questions a teacher must satisfactorily answer before she can arrange a pleasant place for her children:
1. What kind of individuals are meeting here?
2. What is our purpose for children in the church?
Reread Chapters 1 and 2 if the answers do not come clear immediately. For it is basically important that the place or room fit the people and the purpose, if the experiences they have in it are going to be natural and wholesome and make them want to come for more.
Our purpose in guiding boys and girls into becoming disciples of Jesus cannot be achieved in a formal setting where children are expected to "sit in a circle and be good." How can they ever learn to think, to love, to get along with others, if they are sitting still, or standing, marching, going to tables, in an adult-directed fashion all the hour? With pictures too high to see, let alone feel? With much furniture in the way?

48

There are some church members who will say: "The whole hour should be Bible and worship. No need for play and toys." How little they understand the nature of the kindergarten child and how he acts and learns in becoming a Christian! Moreover, there are very sobering statistics that show that many boys and girls who began in the church school when they were young "go out the back door" of the church when they have reached the ages of eleven to thirteen and are lost to the church. Somewhere along the line poor teaching —which includes an unattractive, chilling room—numbed and eventually killed their interest. The local church did not make a good positive impression on them. It had neither the challenge nor enabling vision that rightfully belong to it by virtue of its magnetic, dynamic Christ.

Something of the problem of a cramped spirit can be illustrated by the experience of a four-year-old who was trying to draw a picture of a house during a church school session. She was very hesitant, tight like a knot; she could not start her drawing with freedom as did the other children. Finally, after two stiff lines were made, she put down her crayon emphatically and said: "No wonder I can't do it. My mommie has showed me so many times I haven't learned it for myself."

Children need a place of their own, a place that offers them opportunities to learn for themselves. Once again, children learn by doing!

A ROOM WITH CHILD APPEAL

The place for the kindergarten department in the church building may vary considerably in small and large churches. But understanding adults will persist until they provide a place, whether a room or a corner. Either place, large or small, if it is suitable for the kindergarten, must be:

1. Clean and neat.
2. Inviting to four- and five-year-olds, with things that fit, things on eye level, things to handle.
3. Provide a place for wraps.
4. Have natural light, if at all possible.
5. Show pretty, soft colors.
6. Have movable fixings.

With Chapters 1 and 2 in mind, think of the space in your church or go there on a weekday. Stand at the entry where the children come in each Sunday. It may be at the place between two curtains or around back of the piano. Sit down on your heels or kneel so that your eyes are about as far from the floor as those of the children. Look and look. Do you see:

1. Things with which to play house?
   Dolls (not all the same skin color as the children who use them)
   A broom or carpet sweeper
   A toy telephone
   A pocketbook or shopping bag
   Baskets
   Dishes
   Picture book for baby

   The quantity and variety depend upon the size of the place and the number of children who occupy it.

2. Things with which to build?
   Blocks—as big as space permits, various shapes
   Blocks that fit together well for building can be made from light-weight "two by four" lumber after this pattern:
   a. a square block
   b. twice as long
   c. four times as long
   d. diagonals of a, b, and c
   e. horizontals of a, b, and c
   f. round pillars—1½'' diam. and length of block #b; 3'' diam. and length of block #b
   g. curves, suitable for church doorways
   The sharp edges must be sanded. Sizes, a, b, and c would be used for about 60 per cent or more of the total number.

   Sets of blocks may be purchased from the companies listed at the end of the chapter.
   Boxes
   Cardboard

3. Things needed with the building?
   Cars—milk truck, grocery truck, fire engine, hauling truck, tractor
   Boats
   Airplanes
   People and animals (manufactured of wood, or made with paper figures mounted on cardboard and tacked to a block of wood for standing purposes)

   Again quantity and variety depend on size of space and number of children. Also the community environment of the children, namely, ferryboats are essential to children who see and use them while they are not important to other children.

4. Pictures and books to explore?
   A Bible used frequently by the teacher.
   Pictures if good in quality and from recommended lists.
   Both pictures and books that will help to develop the teaching purposes of the curriculum materials, such as

   Books:
   In the Morning: Twenty Bible Verses. Illustrated by Louise Drew. Abingdon Press, 1947. $1.00.

My Bible Book, by Janie Walker. Rand McNally & Company, 1946.
75 cents.
A Child's Grace, photographs by Constance Bannister. E. P. Dutton & Co., Inc., 1948. $2.50.
The New Baby, by Ruth and Harold Shane. Simon and Schuster, Inc., 1948. $1.00.

God's World and Johnny, A Star Shone, Sammy Moves to Brookdale The Little White Church	and other Westminster Press curriculum books for four- and five-year-olds

Manuel, Rosita, Little Playmate Books, Keiko's Birthday, Nezbah's Lamb, Ronnie's Wish,	and other Friendship Press books for nursery and kindergarten age

Pictures:
  Large colored Picture Sets for Kindergarten from The Westminster Press
  Of Such Is the Kingdom of Heaven, by Elsie Anna Wood
  Christ with Children, Cizek School (Artext)
  Magazine pictures mounted, or used in scrapbooks and on posters
  Children and Their Toys Around the World
  Children and Their Pets Around the World
  Children and Their Homes Around the World
  Babies Around the World

5. A place with flowers or a plant and the Bible?
   Also a picture and the offering container.

6. A little place to put a cherished possession and know it will receive attention?
   "Things I wonder about..."
   "Things I like..."
   "Growing things..."
   "Things I think are beautiful...," and others, as encouraged at various times of year.

7. Low shelves?
   For toys and blocks
   For puzzles and rhythm instruments
   For crayons and paper and paste and brushes
   For books and pictures

8. A wastebasket?
   Cleanup time is important

These are some of the things that make a child feel at home in his church, provide situations for learning, invite his curiosity and questions, and make him feel secure.
There are other things that the teacher must think about:

Ventilation
Window guards on high windows (like screen door guards)
Disposable tissues for handkerchiefs
Handy bandages for scratches
Safety pins and thumbtacks
Scotch tape and masking tape
Newspapers or oilcloth for floor work
Mats for resting periods
A "story rug" in sooty cities. It may be a pretty blue sheet, easily
  washed
A canvas to cover rich carpeting when children paint or paste on the
  floor

If these suggestions for a suitable place for four- and five-year-olds were now in picture form, there would be two items missing that most teachers feel are vital. Were chairs and tables missed?

SPACE—SPACE—and more SPACE! That is what is needed for our children who are growing so fast and so awkwardly. A teacher who realized this and had no way in her crowded church to find more space simply decided to use her room in a new way. She had the chairs and tables taken out. She wrote a letter to the parents about the change and asked that the children wear clothes suitable for sitting on the floor. It took the children a while to get used to it, and it was even harder for the teacher. She had to see insecure children "lost" for a Sunday or two because they had no chair to cling to. She had to answer questions from parents whose children "fairly love those little chairs." She had to answer primary teachers who wondered how she could teach without a table. But in time she succeeded in achieving the feeling of freedom in work and play in the group that she longed for. The children kept aprons at the church for paint and clay work and had blankets to sit on at story time in winter weather.

A children's work specialist who lived and traveled in the East and Middle West the first forty years of her life was disappointed when she first visited churches in the South and on the West Coast. She commented: "In this mild climate I am surprised that churches do not utilize the out of doors for their children. Some of them have patios, but they are for adults. How lovely a patio would be just off the kindergarten room, so that the children could go and come easily and learn much from the freedom of space!" She visualized some pavement there, some growing grass, flowers, trees, and bushes. She saw a bird bath too. And toys that are work materials in the out of doors. Of course the room that bordered such a patio would have large, low windows with clear glass panes.

MAKING THE MOST OF WHAT YOU HAVE

Children's rooms in many churches today, because of the great up-swing in birth rates during the past decade, are badly crowded.

Every church should honestly face the fact of overcrowding, appreciate that the problem will be with it for a long time, and act to remedy it. Basically this means one or more of three alternatives: build additional educational rooms; make alterations within the present building to create more space for children; or effect a "swap" with some older group that has more space than it really needs.

Right as these suggestions are, they often take time to work out. Also there is another approach, namely, making the most of what you have.

It is the observation of professional workers in Christian education that most teachers do not use <u>well</u> the space that they have. Often it is helpful to a teacher to see her room on paper. For instance, figure 1 shows a room used with kindergarten children.

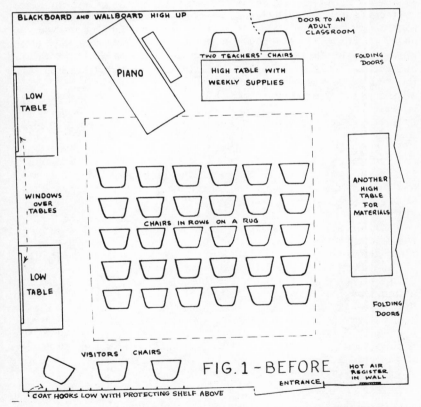

A new teacher who wanted to use the space to better advantage analyzed what furniture was in the room that she did not need. She had the two large tables removed, the legs of the other shortened, and purchased a tall cabinet to hold all the supplies. She removed the teachers' chairs and used two of the children's small chairs at either end of the piano bench, which became a table to hold the Bible, the special picture for the day, offering plate, and flowers. She put the visitors' chairs in the corner formerly unused, which left open space for the removal of wraps. The blackboard was removed, so that it could be used to better advantage with an older class, and the wallboard was placed down on the eye level of kindergarten children. With the help of parents and church school superintendent, she secured two dolls and a doll bed, chair, clothes, dishes, and broom for a housekeeping corner. Later the school bought educational blocks, a loading truck, and a milk truck. A painted orange crate made a bookcase for picture books. A folding screen was arranged by the piano, so that the adults could get into their room without going through the kindergarten room. Most of the chairs were removed, in order to have more space to move around for work and play. The children sat on the rug for group conversation, worship, and story time. The room then looked as shown in figure 2.

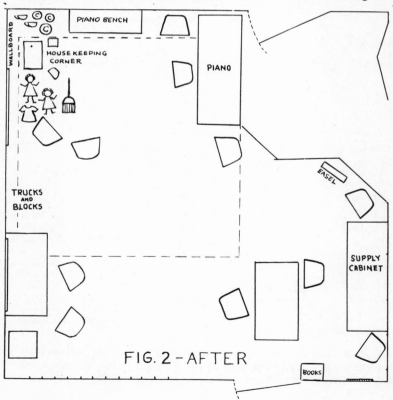

FIG. 2 – AFTER

A discerning teacher who started a private school planned her room much as a salesman does, thinking of his customers, "anticipating the short reach of little arms, the tendency of piled-up objects to fall down and frighten a shy child away, the reluctance of a small child to hunt for something he needs. I made it all as easy and inviting as I knew how, and then I stood aside and let them forage for themselves."[1]

Whether in beautiful room or small corner, the child's real hunger is to live in an atmosphere called Christian, where patience is manifested in the actions and words of adults, and tempers are controlled, where justice is observed and adult mistakes admitted, where love is. For "where love is, there God is also."

To the Reader:

Do be original in the room you use with your children! Do seek expert advice from professional workers in your area. Some teachers report such novel devices as:

Fastening pictures with paper clips on to coat hangers, and putting the hangers on the back of a pew where the children can see them from the pew in which they have to meet.

Hanging draperies to cover up a window or unused door.

Pinning pictures on curtains or attaching them to a stretched wire with snap clothespins or paper clips.

Using chair seats as tables, with children kneeling on floor.

Using shelves for table work, the shelves hinged to the wall and which drop down against the wall when not in use.

Putting coat hooks on the back of the piano, which is moved out from the wall to make a kind of coatroom. Or covering the back of the piano with an appropriate drapery on which pictures may be pinned.

FOR YOUR READING

Education in the Kindergarten, by Josephine Foster and Neith Headley. American Book Company. $4.75.

Equipment and Arrangement for Children's Groups, by Emma Jane Kramer. The Methodist Publishing House. 25 cents.

The Fives and Sixes Go to School, by Emma Dickson Sheehy. Henry Holt & Co., Inc. 1954. $5.00.

How to Make Church School Equipment, by Thelma Adair and Elizabeth McCort. The Westminster Press. $1.25.

Portfolio on Materials for Work and Play. Association for Childhood Education International, 1200 Fifteenth Street, N.W., Washington 5, D. C. 75 cents.

Religion in the Kindergarten, by Rosemary K. Roorbach. Harper & Brothers, 1949, $2.00.

Working with Large Groups of Fours and Fives. Association for Childhood Education International, 1200 Fifteenth Street, N.W., Washington 5, D. C.

---

[1] Page 31 in I Learn from Children, by Caroline Pratt. Simon and Schuster, Inc., 1948.

Catalogues or list prices on various sets of building blocks may be secured from: Educational Equipment Company, 69 West Twenty-third Street, New York, New York, and Macedonia Co-op Community, Clarksville, Georgia.

6. THE TEACHER'S USE OF
PRINTED MATERIALS

Dear Reader:

Have you ever studied your Sunday church school materials and then, instead of teaching, gone to visit another teacher using the same materials? Try it sometime soon. You may discover that: (1) She used it differently from the way you would have used it; (2) She used it better than you would have; or (3) She did not use it as well as you would have used it.

How would you reply in informal conversation to these two people:

1. A teacher was inviting another teacher to take a Leadership Training course with her. The reply to the invitation was: "Why who'd think of studying how to teach a Sunday church school class? Anyone can do that who has grown up in the church."

2. A mother said, "I watched the kindergarten teacher once when I took Ginny, and because she didn't have a plan and do anything definite, I decided that the Presbyterian materials weren't any good."

Writers of our curriculum are skilled teachers of long years of experience with the age for which they write. They know hundreds and thousands of children or young people of a given age. They can estimate what reactions should come from young learners to their written curriculum, because they build it on both the principles of basic Christian aims and also the needs, interests, and capabilities of the particular age group. But one thing they cannot know is what reactions will come from young learners, because the written curriculum is used somewhat differently by every teacher who handles it.

It may be used poorly, perhaps only partially or hurriedly read through by the teacher on the Saturday before a Sunday morning session. Or, it may be read halfheartedly by a teacher who has lost the vision of the real possibility of giving children a satisfying way of life. Or, it can be used well because it is studied keenly, adapted to the individuals in the class, and enriched by personal experiences and prayer.

No curriculum material teaches itself. Its effectiveness depends greatly on the skill of the Christian leader using it. Her diligence and interpretation matter, and so does her contagious enthusiasm. What grownup today has not experienced a dull hour in a church school on a given Sunday morning! What adult today has not experienced indifference or boredom in a Bible study class, not because of the written Word, but because of the teacher!

. A kindergarten teacher approached her superintendent asking: "Why don't we have the stories of Daniel in the lions' den and Moses getting the Ten Commandments? Why, my children aren't going to know all those wonderful stories I knew when I was a child. We have the same ones over and over again." She had been teaching four- and five-year-olds for eight years, but no one had ever helped her to see that:

> She had each child only two years.
> She was giving him what he could now understand for everyday living.
> When her children are in the primary department, they will learn more stories from the Bible to help them in everyday living.
> When they become juniors, they will hear stories they have not heard before, because now they are old enough to understand and appreciate more advanced ideas and ideals.

Chapter 2 helps teachers to see that there are six important purposes in the major goal of all church school teachers, and that each purpose is fulfilled in the kindergarten department to the extent that four- and five-year-olds are capable according to God's laws of growth. The basic concern of a kindergarten teacher then becomes: How can I use the printed materials well? Will my children be closer to the goal of discipleship because they have lived awhile with me?

PREPARING TO TEACH

For a kindergarten teacher using the Christian Faith and Life curriculum these are the printed materials needed:

The Bible

The current quarterly reading book for the child, such as A Star Shone, My Book About Jesus, God's World and Johnny Growing, a quarterly magazine for teachers and parents

The songbook When the Little Child Wants to Sing

The annual packet of Kindergarten Teaching Pictures

The annual packet of Kindergarten Activities

It is often a temptation for a teacher to skim through these printed materials and read only those parts she thinks she will actually use with the children. It is also a temptation to read the printed materials on the "installment" plan or piecemeal, that is, session by session or story by story when the Sunday arrives on which the material will be used. Putting aside such temptations, the thoughtful teacher will prepare herself in these ways:

A. She will constantly work on deepening her own faith by continuous Bible study, prayer, attendance at church worship and reading of recommended books. She realizes that everything she says and does is based on what she believes and feels toward God and man. If she would be the kind of person fit to lead young children in the church, then she must be constantly working to grow in her Christian faith and understanding. For she will unconsciously reflect what she believes! This means too that she will:

1. Read all the Biblical passages given in Growing as the basis for each weekly session and an interpretation of these passages as given in "For the Thinking of Parents and Teachers" at the beginning of each session.

2. Look for the article in each issue of Growing that deals with Biblical and theological understandings. When ideas are difficult to grasp, a teacher can ask the pastor to help her or a group to discuss the article.

3. Ask for a "sabbatical year" or half year when she can join the adult Bible class in their Sunday morning study.

4. Attend a leadership training school and take courses in Bible and theology, as well as courses in teaching kindergarten children.

B. When she studies she will always keep in mind that she is a co-worker with God. Here is a real privilege—to be a "child of God" herself, to know him as companion-guide, to reach out to young children for him. She feels it urgent that she share his love with others, that she be loyal to him by giving her best abilities and time to his work. Then she will ask herself each Sunday, "Did these children come closer to the goal of discipleship because of this hour with me?"

C. She will look at the four- and five-year-old children in her department and ask, "How much can they absorb and understand?" Each quarterly reading book and every issue of Growing are written and edited by people who know what kindergarten boys and girls can comprehend. But if a teacher is a mother she often thinks of what her own child can understand, what he likes and what he dislikes. She is apt to judge all children by the one she knows best. If a teacher has no weekday contact with children she often thinks they cannot do this or are not interested in doing that. Reading books about "what children are like" will help all teachers to understand their many differences and similarities, their basic interests, their ready abilities. Calling in their homes and visiting in their schools gives personal information to a teacher and deepens her concern for each child.

These three ways of preparing oneself to teach are not often mentioned when a person is asked to become a teacher. But these are the sure foundation every teacher must constantly build into her life.

The thought of meeting children each Sunday morning makes teachers realize that they have to "study the lesson." What is "the lesson?" It is guiding boys and girls to Christ through experiences, using specific materials to help the teacher realize a specific purpose on a certain day. In order to teach each Sunday a good teacher will do these things:

A. Read the Prospectus published each spring, to discover the year's plan for the kindergarten department as it begins in October. This booklet gives the titles of each Sunday session with the basic Biblical references. Here a teacher can see the whole year at a glance. It is a sort of road map to guide her on the highway with her children. If she understands the plan for the year as well as for the quarter, she will be accumulating materials that will help to enrich the experiences of her individual children in their particular community. A teacher in a large city finds that she has to be ready with many materials from the country—many, many pictures and objects—in order to help her city children know and appreciate God as the source of their food, and also the part the farmer and trucker play. A teacher in the country who is using the same lesson materials in Growing will search for ways to make the commonplace have spiritual reality to her rural boys and girls who are so aware of how food grows.

B. Read the current quarterly reading book for the child, such as A Star Shone, My Book About Jesus, and others. Notice verses and prayers on the inside cover pages.

C. Read Growing as a whole magazine. The latter part of it contains the Sunday plans for three months. To read them through at one sitting gives a teacher a clear idea of what she will be doing for thirteen Sundays.

   1. Look at the two page summary entitled "Outline for This Quarter."

      a. Study the purposes for each session. These are what you aim to accomplish.

      b. Notice the Biblical references given for adult study as well as the short verse for children.

      c. Survey the stories. See what other sources are to be used besides the current reading book for the child.

      d. Study the picture list. Have you filed the kindergarten pictures year by year so that they can be found easily by subject?

    e. Sing the suggested songs at home so you are able to use them readily without having to turn pages or wait for a pianist.

  2. Read "Planning Ahead for the Church School," which gives special help for general work in the department and for certain seasonal Sundays.

  3. Look for the articles that appear in each issue, dealing with Bible study, theology, family life, the child, methods of teaching, missions and social concern, organization of the kindergarten department.

D. Make department lesson plans for the unit or month in co-operation with all the teachers. Elsewhere in this book it has been stated that four- and five-year-olds learn best in a group of 20 to 25 children or less. This means that churches which have 80 to 100 children of this age are dividing them into four kindergarten departments by ages with two meeting at church school time and two at church time. It is not wise to have one large department with several "classes" because children learn best in an informal, homelike atmosphere. The work of a department is done by a superintendent and assistants. All are teachers. Together they make monthly lesson plans and determine:

who tells the story each Sunday

who teaches a new song

who prepares materials for activity time

who reads at the book table

who guides conversation when children place their offering shortly after arrival

who helps when needed in the block corner, in the house corner, at the easel

Children respond more readily and feel at home in a basic routine that is informal, such as that suggested in Growing for each Sunday. The leading teacher should be the same each Sunday with other teachers taking part. Planning ahead makes for smoothness, for each teacher knows her part and the children in turn sense the unity of the hour. Children can always tell whether or not a teacher knows what she is about.

E. Make weekly lesson plans, beginning on Sunday afternoon.

  1. As soon as a Sunday morning session is over a teacher realizes that some things must surely be done the next Sunday. She writes them down immediately, such things as this: promised Junella that she can help put up pictures; Jeffrey visits a dairy farm this week, so be sure to have him tell about it; we did not fulfill our purpose today, so use the same one next Sunday; Tom wants Mrs. B to finish reading The Little Seeds That Grow.

  2. Then she reads the purpose of next Sunday's session and asks, How can I develop this purpose—

in the early informal time of work and play?

in the group time of conversation?

with the four-year-olds in story and activity time?
with the five-year-olds in story and activity time?
3. Is anything new introduced? A new song? A new kind of activity that needs careful guidance?
4. Are special materials needed? Cloth books for making scrapbooks? A clock face of cardboard? Rhythm instruments?
5. Check with each teacher about her responsibility early in the week.

Sometimes when a teacher begins her thinking for next week on Sunday afternoon she realizes that she did not accomplish her purpose with the children that morning. So she decides to have another session with the same purpose, using some new and some of the same materials. Each week she must think in terms of changed attitudes, increased knowledge, and growing skills in her children. This takes time; children cannot be pushed or rushed into learning. So, sometimes the teacher needs to spend two Sundays or more on a purpose that her children need in particular.

The magazine Growing gives suggested outlines for lesson plans with kindergarten children. Also in the week-by-week plans it suggests how the time might be used in proceeding from one item to another. Briefly, it is usually best to start with informal activity and build into group experiences. An experienced teacher will intermingle these so that Bible, music, prayer, pictures, and spontaneous worship all move in and through the session informally. Read again Chapter 3, which describes an informal kindergarten of one hour's length on Sunday morning.

An inexperienced teacher may have to carry her lesson plan with her, written on a small card, so that she can concentrate on leading the children to experience the purpose of the morning. She will need a clock in the room to make her mindful of passing minutes. She will have to learn when informal play can be culminated satisfactorily, or used to further her purpose (recall the way informal play was ended in Chapter 3 and the way it led to worship in Chapter 4, page 34). She will need to learn how to ask questions and handle children's comments, so that conversations will guide the group farther toward achieving the purpose. She will need to study the various techniques or ways of guiding children in Christian growth as well as sense the influence of the environment.

F. Evaluate each Sunday's session. Evaluating what one does in household chores or office work is a common procedure. But evaluating what happens when one is trying to lead a group of active children is a bit more difficult, and much more necessary because many growing lives are involved. Read again pages 26-29 to see how evaluation can be done. As a way of beginning, these questions may be asked:

1. Did I feel happiness within the group? Security? Curiosity?
2. Did I fulfill my purpose?
3. How did my plan fit the four-year-olds? Five-year-olds? Active and quiet periods alternating? Leisurely feeling vs. hurried? Vocabulary used? Questions asked?
4. Did I anticipate responses, so that we moved naturally from song to play to story to Bible to picture to...?
5. Am I in a "rut"? Did we do the same things in the same order?
6. Could I have used Tom's comment instead of ignoring it? Should I have ignored Jane's suggestion instead of using it?
7. Did all the teachers in the room know beforehand what to do?
8. Did I pay enough attention to the parents who visited and who came in at the end?
9. Am I expecting parents to use the magazine without helping them in any way? How can the parents' committee and I help individual families?
10. Do I study and make careful preparations? Am I growing in my devotion to Him, so that in all I do little children are drawn to the Father's love and to the friendship of Jesus?

Printed curriculum materials are only as good as the teachers who use them.

DON'T	DO
Meet a group of children without a purpose and a plan.	Know what you are about; let God use the best self possible.
Force the children to follow your lesson plan as you have it outlined.	Make a plan and use it, but be ready to change it because of children's contributions.
Keep using the same plan.	Remember that children feel secure in a certain amount of routine, but that variety from taking their lead is important.
Fill every minute of your lesson plan with teacher's directions.	Allow time for informality, for free choice of what the child wants to do with the interesting things in the room. Allow time for talking and singing about new shoes, the new baby at home, the sick puppy. Allow time for looking, just looking and feeling things that the children are encouraged to bring: stones, flowers, dolls.

DON'T	DO
Think Sunday morning is the only time you can teach your four- and five-year-olds or that they have to stay in their own room or corner.	Occasionally have a midweek session; every year make sure to hold a vacation church school; have a party or excursion every once in a while; use the out of doors and stores and homes for more learning experiences.

READING THAT WILL HELP

Books listed at the close of Chapter 5.

Design for Teaching—How the Best Church School Teachers Go About Their Work. Division of Christian Education, National Council of Churches of Christ, 257 Fourth Avenue, New York 10, New York. 30 cents.

If I Be His Disciple, by Eda O. Borseth. Board of Christian Education of the Presbyterian Church in the U.S.A. 35 cents.

7. HOW A KINDERGARTEN DEPARTMENT IS MANAGED

Dear Reader:

When one visits a kindergarten room where children are busy in various learning situations, where teachers know what they are about, where parents visit and help, one may be sure that she does not see it all on the surface in that one hour or two hours. Underneath are many details that had to be cared for by someone, details that are never finished but keep moving along day in and day out. What are these important details?

In every business, profession, or factory, there are certain details that have to be taken care of by someone. Big details for the entire work are usually handled by an "executive" and specialized details are done by the "head of the department." In a church school, with its various sections of Sunday, vacation, and weekday church school meetings, the superintendent is generally known as the "executive." But this person cannot possibly handle or know all the important detailed work in each class and department. If there is a small kindergarten group in the church, then the teacher of it has to manage details as well as teach, call in the homes, and keep records. If there is a kindergarten department, there should be a kindergarten superintendent, who is in charge of the details assigned to her secretary; a pianist; assisting teachers; and parents' committee. Whether with a large or small group, the leader of the kindergarten must keep in mind and work hard on three primary things:

Know the children, parents, and homes in which they live.
Make thorough preparation for teaching.
Keep necessary supplies on hand.

Subdivisions under each of these main duties will be necessary according to the local situation.

KNOW THE CHILDREN, PARENTS, HOMES

1. Through written records:
   a. Keep a list at home as well as at the church; some lists take the form of a card file, but all include the following information:

Name	Birth Date
Address	
Phone	
Father's Initials	Church Member
Mother's Name	Church Member
Date Enrolled	
Issues of Reading Book Received	
Issues of Growing Received	
Attendance at Parents' Meetings	

   b. Have a personal record of individual children for teaching purposes, and keep record at home. For example:

   > Billy Smith
   > Just sits when he arrives (I wonder why!)
   > Played trucking business with David when I suggested to David that he ask him on his third Sunday.
   > When asked to help fix wobbly doll cupboard, he measured and found the right-sized block to keep the cupboard firm.
   > Called in home April 20: Billy is youngest, with a sister 15. Mother says he likes painting and books, listens to anything she reads him, is now hearing the Knights of King Arthur.

   Such intimate notes help a teacher over a period of time to know her children individually and to provide learning situations that they seem to need.
   c. Keep accurate records. This is important to the church and to the individual security of the child in a large or new group.
   Remember birthdays. One teacher writes KB on each date on her kitchen calendar when there is a kindergarten birthday, so that she will remember to send a card. Another keeps a "birthday calendar," listing all by months, tacked on her wall so that she can anticipate birthday celebrations.
2. Through personal contacts:
   a. Discover reasons for absences: sickness of child or mother, new baby, a trip, unhappy experience in church school the last time, parental laziness. Each needs friendly concern of teacher.

b. Pay attention to the new child and his family in the community: look for them, encourage children to bring them, visit in the home, tell the minister about them, have a kindergarten parent and child who live nearby visit them. In any church, particularly a larger city one, a letter of welcome immediately from the pastor and superintendent will help make the family feel welcome, perhaps even before a call is possible.

c. Make visitors young or old feel welcome. This may be a "trial" experience for them in your church, or in the Christian church in general.

d. At the beginning of each quarter, or as new pupils are enrolled, give out the child's quarterly reading book for use in the home.

e. Give out Youth Budget pledge cards and envelopes, or see that the Youth Budget Committee has your accurate records for this.

f. Plan regular promotion times.

(1) Kindergarten materials are for four- and five-year-olds, and they do not fit three-year-olds.

Have a special place for three-year-olds: a separate room if at all possible; or at least a corner of the kindergarten room where they work by themselves. This latter arrangement is not the best, but it is better than nothing if a leader thoughtfully plans her work. Some teachers in a small church successfully use one very large room for nursery, kindergarten, and primary children. There are only a few of each age, but they work and play in their own groups, besides having some lovely interchange of friendship, helping, and sharing. For guidance in work with nursery children, read Before They Are Three, by Thompson, Klein, and Gardner, and When They Are Three, by Sara G. Klein.

(2.) Traditionally promotion from the kindergarten to the primary department takes place in most churches in June or in September. Local churches vary considerably in their habits at this point, and also in the extent of regular Sunday church school work during the summer. Promotion from the kindergarten should be integrated with the whole school's plan, and therefore cleared with the general superintendent.

MAKE THOROUGH PREPARATION FOR TEACHING

1. In many localities, this preparation is stimulated by an area curriculum conference or quarterly preview in a presbytery or district. The department head should by all means attend. Such an area conference is not to be thought of as a substitute for a pre-

view and lesson planning conference in the local church, but a
preparation for it. The matters discussed in Chapter 6 are very
pertinent at this point. The size of kindergarten groups will
vary, but the following will suggest what should be done locally:

a. If, for example, a kindergarten teacher has but five children in
her class, she will need only to have a quarterly preview with
the parents, which ought to occur each quarter within the
period of several weeks before the start of the quarter. It
has been found that meeting in the home of one couple will
best attract other parents.

b. If, on the other hand, there is a kindergarten department with
twenty children, it might well have a superintendent, plus two
assisting teachers, and some key parents or a committee of
them. In this case the superintendent and teachers, with the
key parents or committee, would first need to hold their own
"huddle" to think through their plans for the quarter's work.
Only after this would they hold a preview for all the parents
of the department.

c. If, as a further example, there is a church with a kindergarten
department of from fifty to seventy children, the kindergarten
superintendent would probably have about six regular assisting
teachers, two substitutes, a pianist, and a secretary. In this
circumstance she will have a teachers' or departmental preview and lesson planning conference with all ten leaders plus
a key parent (or father and a mother) from each neighborhood
of about ten families. They in turn might well plan neighborhood parent meetings to highlight and discuss the contents of
the magazine Growing, their children's home reading book,
and the means of making all family living more Christian.
Questions about growth in prayer, behavior problems, and
major theological puzzlers that youngsters pose should be
answered.

With a department as large as this, a wise superintendent, if
space permits, will divide her kindergarten group into a four-
year-old group and a five-year-old group, with separate
rooms if possible. When a group consists of more than twenty,
happiness and good learning opportunities decrease.

2. What is a parents' committee?

If in our church school work we would think and act in terms of
families, the church would make a greater impact on society.
For it is in the family that the individual learns the most about
living, and does the most of his living in impressionable years.
Every kindergarten teacher recognizes the importance of the
home, but not everyone uses some of her children's parents to
reach other parents. In Chapter 3, an active parents' committee
was at work doing certain things that week. Here are other things
they can do:

Make doll clothes and bedding.
Keep toys and dolls washed and clean.
Keep books in good repair.
Keep library system for lending books.
Paint furniture or walls when needed.
Hunt for magazine pictures to illustrate particular subjects.
Help mount teaching pictures.
Call in homes. This is the "Five-Star" Duty.
Sort activity packet sheets in September.
Deliver magazines and explain them to parents who could not attend the
parent preview. So Important!
Help with snow suits, if necessary, in wintertime.
Help as substitutes or assistants in teaching.
Plan informal parent meetings for discussing four- and five-year-olds.
Plan a rotating library of good books and leaflets for other parents.

KEEP NECESSARY SUPPLIES ON HAND

The superintendent of a kindergarten needs to be a good house-keeper, not in the sense of being a fuss-budget, but in the sense of having things ready when and where they are needed. She will keep a scrupulously clean, orderly supply shelf or cupboard. And the children will need low shelves or painted orange crates as places to keep the things that are theirs.

Materials, as suggested earlier in Chapter 5, need not be expensive, but they definitely should be on hand and ready for use when needed. The following list includes the most necessary items:

1. Educational toys (as listed in Chapter 5) may be solicited from children who are nine or ten and have outgrown their kindergarten toys.
2. Clay. Dry powder clay is more economical, for it can be mixed as needed. Order from a school supply house.
3. Paper. Newsprint, wall, shelf, butcher, wrapping, and some colored construction for mounting pictures or for use as "doilies" under flowers or special objects.
4. Paint. Powder or poster paint from school supply houses.
5. Crayons. Not a box for each child (which prevents sharing and taking of turns), nor just a heap of leftover broken bits. Buy a few good kindergarten crayons one half inch in diameter.
6. Paste and glue, and wet rags handy for wiping hands that have used them.
7. Scissors. Seldom used; a few good ones are better than many small, stiff ones.

ARE YOU A GOOD MANAGER?

Every teacher often wishes that she might know how she is progressing in her work. Chapter 6 suggested certain questions to ask in evaluation of one's own teaching. These questions might be asked in further evaluating the management of a department:

1. Whose ideas get used in the kindergarten room? The superintendent's only? Or those of all the teachers, children, and parents?
2. Is there a feeling of frankness and understanding in making suggestions to one another?
3. Does each person follow through in doing assigned work?
4. Is the opinion of the pastor or director asked for?
5. What magazines and books have been read the past six months that
   bear on church school work?
6. Any Leadership Training courses attended? Or Laboratory School
   in summer?
7. Is the leader really trying to know and understand those who are
   sometimes called "problem children"?

Even in the details of administration as listed here, there is a
clear-cut message to the kindergarten teacher:

The individual is important in the eyes of God. A birthday is an
individual's day. New or sick or unhappy children have individual
needs. Working with other teachers who do not always see things
the same way reveals individual viewpoints. Working with the
minister, superintendent, officers in whole-church affairs calls for
individuals working together.

A person matures as a Christian to the extent that all life is lived
in the spirit of Christ.

Dear Reader:

If you have chosen to be a kindergarten teacher, you will soon come
upon many obstacles. You will find that your class is far too large
for the room assigned to it; that it will be difficult to find space to play
with blocks or draw or paint; that you have to get some materials
ready six months in advance, such as a cocoon or special flower bulbs;
that you have to lug the department's growing things home every week
to keep them warm and watered and return with them on Sundays. You
will observe that the teacher of adults does not have so much lugging
and hunting. You will have parents who want to know why you do not
teach all the songs they learned when they were little. Yes, and sometimes you will hear from some adults: "You teach the kindergarten?
That must be easy. I really have to study for my young people's class."

But in spite of these and many other obstacles, you will so sincerely
believe in the importance of early impressions and Christian learning
that you will want to help four- and five-year-olds in the church. So it
is that the obstacles make you call upon all your resources and origin-
ality, make you study every helpful book with discernment, make you
think about your Sunday work all during the week while doing homely
chores, make you remember to keep close to God in prayer in regard
to your difficulties and your joys.

For in this work you are an active disciple of Christ, and a co-worker
with him.